THE ASSASSINATION
Death of the President

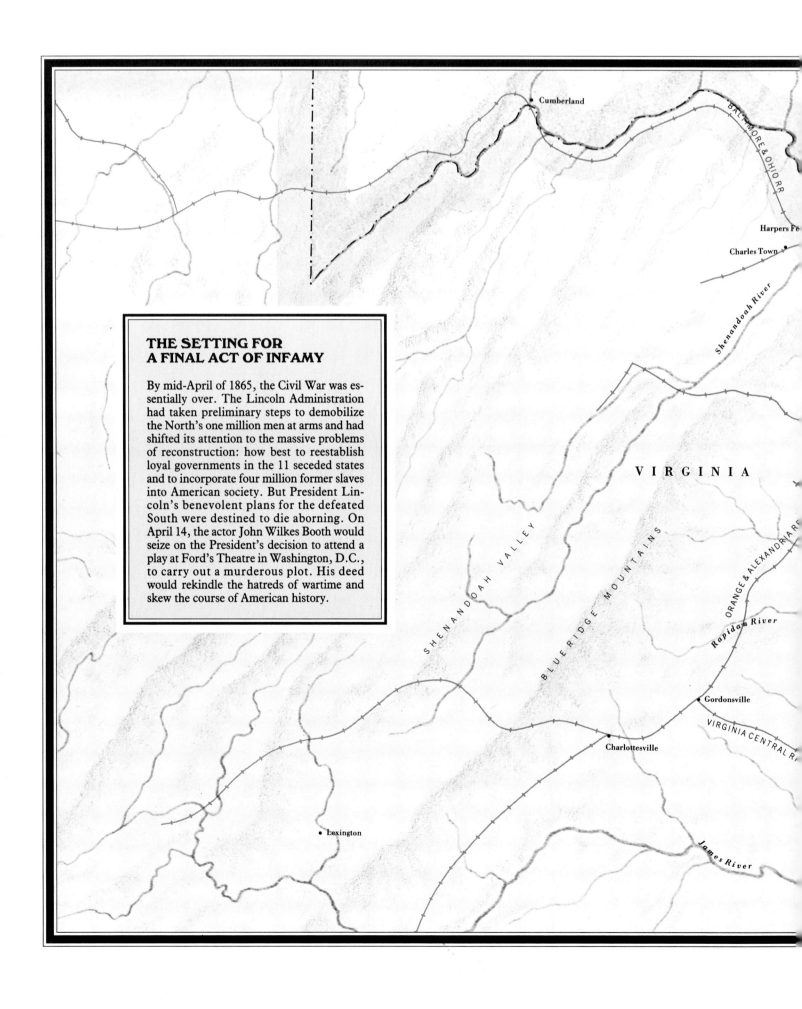

THE SETTING FOR
A FINAL ACT OF INFAMY

By mid-April of 1865, the Civil War was essentially over. The Lincoln Administration had taken preliminary steps to demobilize the North's one million men at arms and had shifted its attention to the massive problems of reconstruction: how best to reestablish loyal governments in the 11 seceded states and to incorporate four million former slaves into American society. But President Lincoln's benevolent plans for the defeated South were destined to die aborning. On April 14, the actor John Wilkes Booth would seize on the President's decision to attend a play at Ford's Theatre in Washington, D.C., to carry out a murderous plot. His deed would rekindle the hatreds of wartime and skew the course of American history.

Cumberland

Harpers Fe

Charles Town

Shenandoah River

VIRGINIA

SHENANDOAH VALLEY

BLUE RIDGE MOUNTAINS

ORANGE & ALEXANDRIA R

Rapidan River

Gordonsville

VIRGINIA CENTRAL R

Charlottesville

BALTIMORE & OHIO RR

Lexington

James River

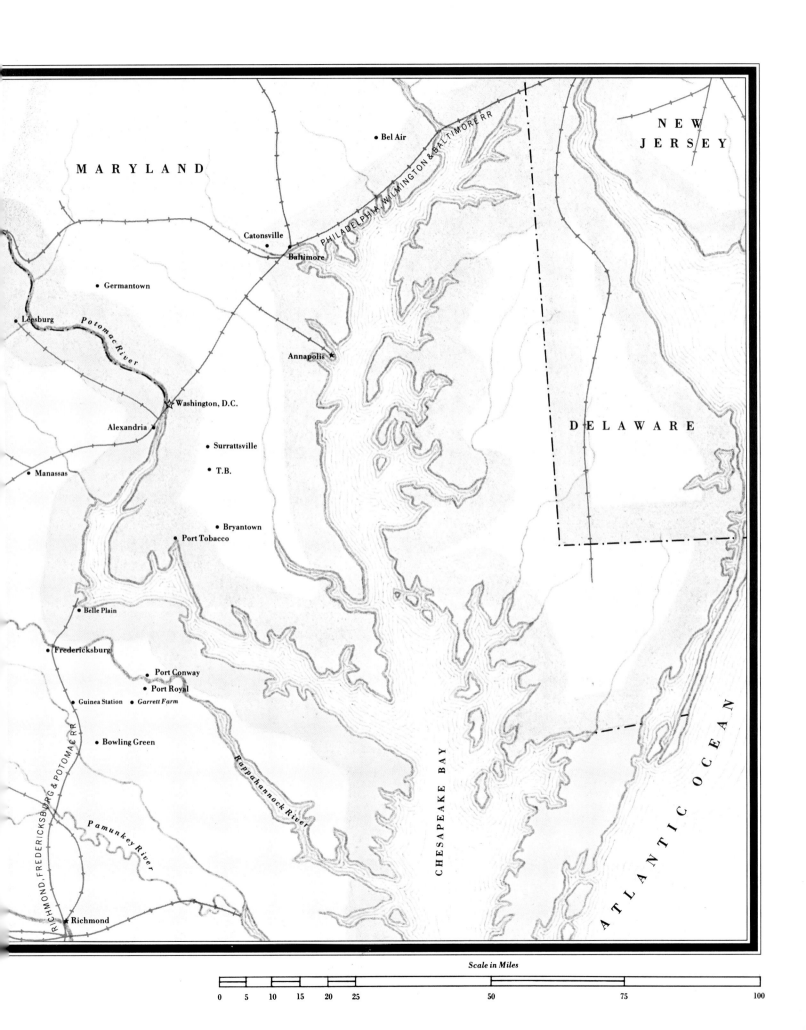

NEW
JERSEY

MARYLAND

Bel Air

PHILADELPHIA, WILMINGTON & BALTIMORE RR

Catonsville

Baltimore

Germantown

Leesburg

Potomac River

Annapolis

DELAWARE

Washington, D.C.

Alexandria

Surrattsville

Manassas

T.B.

Bryantown

Port Tobacco

Belle Plain

Fredericksburg

Port Conway

Port Royal

Guinea Station

Garrett Farm

Bowling Green

Rappahannock River

CHESAPEAKE BAY

RICHMOND, FREDERICKSBURG & POTOMAC RR

Pamunkey River

Richmond

ATLANTIC OCEAN

Scale in Miles

0   5   10   15   20   25   50   75   100

TIME® LIFE BOOKS

Other Publications:

THE TIME-LIFE GARDENER'S GUIDE
MYSTERIES OF THE UNKNOWN
TIME FRAME
FIX IT YOURSELF
FITNESS, HEALTH & NUTRITION
SUCCESSFUL PARENTING
HEALTHY HOME COOKING
UNDERSTANDING COMPUTERS
LIBRARY OF NATIONS
THE ENCHANTED WORLD
THE KODAK LIBRARY OF CREATIVE PHOTOGRAPHY
GREAT MEALS IN MINUTES
PLANET EARTH
COLLECTOR'S LIBRARY OF THE CIVIL WAR
THE EPIC OF FLIGHT
THE GOOD COOK
WORLD WAR II
HOME REPAIR AND IMPROVEMENT
THE OLD WEST

For information on and a full description of any of the
Time-Life Books series listed above, please call 1-800-621-
7026 or write:
Reader Information
Time-Life Customer Service
P.O. Box C-32068
Richmond, Virginia 23261-2068

This volume is one of a series that chronicles in full the
events of the American Civil War, 1861-1865.
Other books in the series include:

The Cover: Three years of war were over, but some of
the worst bloodshed was still to come when this photograph of a resolute Abraham Lincoln was made in
early 1864. "Mr. Lincoln," noted a British observer,
"is perhaps the only man in the North who has never
wavered, doubted, or abated of heart or hope. He
has always been calm, confident, determined, the
type and embodiment of the national will."

THE
CIVIL
WAR

THE ASSASSINATION

BY

CHAMP CLARK

AND THE

EDITORS OF TIME-LIFE BOOKS

Death of the President

TIME-LIFE BOOKS, ALEXANDRIA, VIRGINIA

Time-Life Books Inc.
is a wholly owned subsidiary of
TIME INCORPORATED

FOUNDER: Henry R. Luce 1898-1967

Editor-in-Chief: Henry Anatole Grunwald
Chairman and Chief Executive Officer: J. Richard Munro
President and Chief Operating Officer: N. J. Nicholas Jr.
Chairman of the Executive Committee: Ralph P. Davidson
Corporate Editor: Ray Cave
Executive Vice President, Books: Kelso F. Sutton
Vice President, Books: George Artandi

TIME-LIFE BOOKS INC.

EDITOR: George Constable
Executive Editor: Ellen Phillips
Director of Design: Louis Klein
Director of Editorial Resources: Phyllis K. Wise
Editorial Board: Russell B. Adams Jr., Thomas H.
Flaherty, Lee Hassig, Donia Ann Steele, Rosalind
Stubenberg, Kit van Tulleken, Henry Woodhead
Director of Photography and Research:
John Conrad Weiser

PRESIDENT: Christopher T. Linen
Chief Operating Officer: John M. Fahey Jr.
Senior Vice Presidents: James L. Mercer,
Leopoldo Toralballa
Vice Presidents: Stephen L. Bair, Ralph J. Cuomo, Neal
Goff, Stephen L. Goldstein, Juanita T. James, Hallett
Johnson III, Robert H. Smith, Paul R. Stewart
Director of Production Services: Robert J. Passantino

The Civil War
Series Director: Thomas H. Flaherty
Designer: Edward Frank
Series Administrator: Jane Edwin

Editorial Staff for *The Assassination*
Associate Editors: R. W. Murphy, David S. Thomson
(text); Jane N. Coughran (pictures)
Staff Writers: Janet Cave, Margery A. duMond,
John Newton, Brian C. Pohanka
Researchers: Kristin Baker, Gwen Mullen (principals);
Jane A. Martin
Assistant Designer: Lorraine D. Rivard
Copy Coordinator: Vivian Noble
Picture Coordinator: Betty H. Weatherley
Editorial Assistant: Donna Fountain
Special Contributors: Roxie France-Nuriddin,
Brian E. McGinn, William Alan Pitts

Editorial Operations
Copy Chief: Diane Ullius
Editorial Operations Manager: Caroline A. Boubin
Production: Celia Beattie
Quality Control: James J. Cox (director)
Library: Louise D. Forstall

Correspondents: Elisabeth Kraemer-Singh (Bonn);
Maria Vincenza Aloisi (Paris); Ann Natanson (Rome).
Valuable assistance was also provided by: Fran Youssef
(Dallas); Elizabeth Brown, Christina Lieberman
(New York).

Library of Congress Cataloguing in Publication Data
Clark, Champ.
    The assassination: the death of the president.
    (The Civil War)
    Bibliography: p.
    Includes index.
    1. Lincoln, Abraham, 1809-1865 — Assassination.
I. Time-Life Books.   II. Title.   III. Series.
E457.5.C6 1987   973.7'092'4   87-1899
    ISBN 0-8094-4820-3
    ISBN 0-8094-4821-1 (lib. bdg.)

The Author:
Champ Clark, a veteran of 23 years as a correspondent,
writer and senior editor for *Time*, retired from weekly
journalism in 1972 in order to freelance and to teach in the
English Department at the University of Virginia. He is
the author of numerous Time-Life books, including *The
Badlands* in the American Wilderness series, *Flood* in the
Planet Earth series and *Decoying the Yanks* and *Gettysburg*
in the Civil War series.

The Consultants:
Terry Alford is Professor of History at Northern Virginia
Community College, Annandale, Virginia. He was curator of an exhibition on the 120th anniversary of the Lincoln assassination, held at Georgetown University Library, and is the author of the exhibition catalogue, *This
One Mad Act*. He teaches a course on the assassination
each semester at Georgetown University. He is the author
of *Prince among Slaves* and is currently researching the life
of John Wilkes Booth.

Colonel John R. Elting, USA (Ret.), a former Associate
Professor at West Point, is the author of *Battles for Scandi-
navia* in the Time-Life Books World War II series and of
The Battle of Bunker's Hill, *The Battles of Saratoga*, *Military History and Atlas of the Napoleonic Wars*, *American
Army Life* and *The Superstrategists*. Co-author of *A Dic-
tionary of Soldier Talk*, he is also editor of the three vol-
umes of *Military Uniforms in America, 1755-1867*, and associate editor of *The West Point Atlas of American Wars*.

William A. Frassanito, a Civil War historian and lecturer
specializing in photograph analysis, is the author of two
award-winning studies, *Gettysburg: A Journey in Time* and
*Antietam: The Photographic Legacy of America's Bloodiest
Day*, and a companion volume, *Grant and Lee, The Virginia Campaigns*. He has also served as chief consultant to the
photographic history series *The Image of War*.

Les Jensen, Director of the Second Armored Division
Museum, Fort Hood, Texas, specializes in Civil War arti-
facts and is a conservator of historic flags. He is a contribu-
tor to *The Image of War* series, consultant for numerous
Civil War publications and museums, and a member of
the Company of Military Historians. He was formerly Curator of the U.S. Army Transportation Museum at Fort
Eustis, Virginia, and before that Curator of the Museum
of the Confederacy in Richmond, Virginia.

Michael McAfee specializes in military uniforms and has
been Curator of Uniforms and History at the West Point
Museum since 1970. A fellow of the Company of Military
Historians, he coedited with Colonel Elting *Long Endure:
The Civil War Years*, and he collaborated with Frederick
Todd on *American Military Equipage*. He is the author of
Artillery of the American Revolution, 1775-1783 and has
written numerous articles for *Military Images Magazine*.

James P. Shenton, Professor of History at Columbia University, is a specialist in 19th-century American political
and social history, with particular emphasis on the Civil
War period. He is the author of *Robert John Walker* and
Reconstruction South.

CONTENTS

A Haunting Dream

"It would never do for a President to have guards with drawn sabres at his door, as if he fancied he were, or were trying to be, an emperor."

ABRAHAM LINCOLN

In the days and nights following Robert E. Lee's surrender at Appomattox, the Union erupted in a star-spangled celebration of waving flags and chiming church bells, patriotic speeches and torchlight parades. Perhaps more than any man alive, Abraham Lincoln had reason to share in the nation's joy. Yet on the evening of April 11, 1865, as the President and his wife entertained their old Illinois friend Ward Hill Lamon and several other acquaintances in the Red Room of the White House, Lincoln appeared to be almost melancholy.

Lamon, who later wrote down Lincoln's words, recalled that the President mused on the subject of dreams and on a nightmare he had had a few evenings earlier. "It seems strange," Lincoln began, "how much there is in the Bible about dreams. There are, I think, some 16 chapters in the Old Testament and four or five in the New in which dreams are mentioned." Believers in the Bible, the President continued, "must accept the fact that in the old days God and His angels came to men in their sleep and made themselves known in dreams."

Then, as if to dismiss the subject, he ruefully added: "Nowadays, dreams are regarded as very foolish, and are seldom told, except by old women and young men and maidens in love."

But Mary Todd Lincoln, who had been afflicted since childhood by dreadful nightmares, would not let the subject drop. Did her husband truly believe in dreams?

"I can't say that I do," Lincoln replied, "but I had one the other night which has haunted me ever since."

"You frighten me," said Mrs. Lincoln. "What is the matter?"

By now the President evidently regretted having aroused the morbid fears that sprang from his wife's anxious nature. "I am afraid that I have done wrong to mention the subject at all," he said. "But somehow the thing has got possession of me, and, like Banquo's ghost, it will not down."

Despite her husband's obvious reluctance, Mrs. Lincoln insisted that he describe the nagging nightmare, and at last he agreed. One recent night he had gone wearily to bed after waiting up late for important dispatches. Almost immediately he had fallen into a deep slumber and soon had begun to dream. "There seemed to be a deathlike stillness about me," he said. "Then I heard subdued sobs, as if a number of people were weeping. I thought I left my bed and wandered downstairs."

Finding no one, he roamed from room to room seeking the source of the sorrowing sounds. "I kept on," he continued, "until I arrived in the East Room, which I entered. There I met with a sickening surprise. Before me was a catafalque, on which rested a corpse in funeral vestments. Around it were stationed soldiers who were acting as guards; and there was a throng of people, some gazing mournfully upon the corpse, whose face was covered, others weeping pitifully.

Abraham Lincoln sat for this photograph in February 1865. Only one print was made from the glass negative, which broke during developing.

" 'Who is dead in the White House?' I demanded of one of the soldiers.

" 'The President,' was his answer. 'He was killed by an assassin!' "

The hush that fell upon the little gathering was broken at length by Mrs. Lincoln.

"That is horrid," she said. "I wish you had not told it."

The President was consoling. "It was only a dream, Mary," he said. "Let us say no more about it and try to forget it."

For Abraham Lincoln's nightmare to become reality would require an act of violence running against the tide of American history. Of the 15 men who had preceded Lincoln as President of the United States, all had died of natural causes. Only one, Andrew Jackson, had been an assassin's target — and Jackson's life had been spared when the pistols wielded by the would-be killer, an insane house painter, both misfired. Lincoln's Secretary of State, William H. Seward, noted proudly that the record of orderly presidential succession was a cause for national self-congratulation. "Assassination," he declared, "is not an American practice or habit, and one so vicious and so desperate cannot be engrafted into our political system."

The Civil War, however, had been a massive upheaval that had overturned traditional values; from its convulsive hatreds had risen the clear possibility of violence directed at the President. Even before the War began, Maryland secessionists had made a plan to murder Lincoln as he passed through Baltimore on the way to his inauguration. The conspirators were talkative, however, and Federal detectives got wind of the plot in time to smuggle the President-elect safely through the city and on to Washington.

Poisonous letters, the products of minds inflamed by the issues dividing the nation, had begun to appear soon after Lincoln's nomination. Some were pure rant, such as the letter addressed to "Old Abe Lincoln" by someone who signed himself "Pete Muggins." It began: "God damn your god damned old Hellfired god damned soul to Hell." Others, although less blasphemous, were more explicitly menacing. Once war broke out, a steady flow of letters threatening violence arrived at the White House. The President's secretaries apparently destroyed scores of the malicious messages before Lincoln could see them. Even so, by March of 1865 a large envelope that the President kept in his desk — and on which he had written the word "Assassination" — contained no fewer than 80 threats to his life.

For the most part, Lincoln took a fatalistic attitude toward the perils of his position. "I cannot possibly guard myself against all dangers," he once remarked, "unless I shut myself up in an iron box, in which condition I could scarcely perform the duties of a President." He went on to say, "If anyone is willing to give his life for mine, there is nothing that can prevent it."

Only chance had prevented Lincoln's assassination in the summer of 1862. A bullet fired by an unseen assailant — who was never caught — smashed through the President's top hat as he was riding to an asylum for disabled veterans of the Regular Army called the Soldiers' Home, which was situated on a lonely road three miles north of Washington.

By the summer of 1864, with Lee's troops penned into the trenches around Petersburg, Virginia, the willingness of Southern sympathizers to take revenge on the President had intensified in proportion to the South's fail-

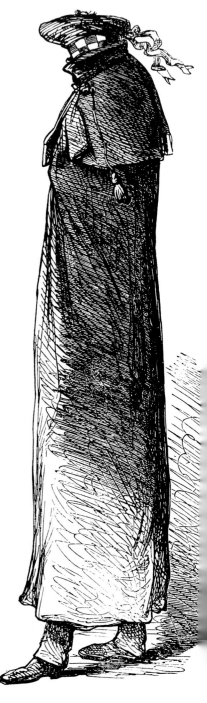

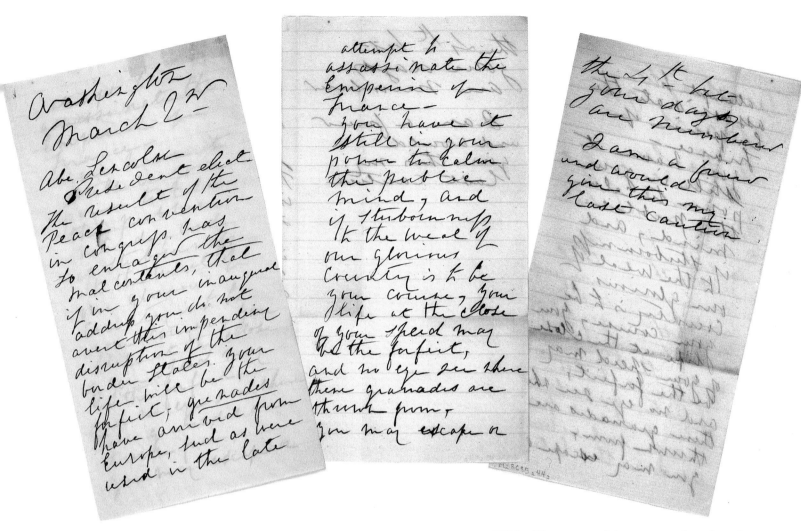

One of the early written threats against Lincoln's life was the 1861 letter shown above. The anonymous author vows to throw grenades at Lincoln during his inauguration if the new President does not act immediately to "avert the impending disruption" of the Union.

Lincoln was sensitive to published insinuations that he feared for his life. The sketch at left, depicting him wrapped in a long coat and cap, appeared in *Vanity Fair* after Lincoln slipped furtively through Baltimore in 1861, foiling a reported plot to kill him while he was on the way to his first inauguration.

ing prospects. Advertisements in Southern newspapers offered large sums to anyone who succeeded in killing the President. An Alabaman named George Washington Gayle placed an advertisement vowing that if his fellow Southerners would subscribe $1 million, he would see to it that Lincoln met a violent end. Government detectives in Washington heard rumors of plots to murder or abduct the President. So did Lincoln's crony Ward Hill Lamon, who had been appointed marshal of the District of Columbia and considered himself the President's chief bodyguard. Among the others increasingly fearful for Lincoln's life was Secretary of War Edwin M. Stanton.

The President tended to laugh off their warnings. On one occasion he called Lamon "a monomaniac on the subject of my safety." Nevertheless, Lincoln finally agreed to take some precautions. On the second floor of the White House, partitions were placed so that the President could walk from his bedroom to his office without having to run the gauntlet of office-seekers who usually thronged the corridor — or the potential assassins who might be amid them. On social occasions at the White House, guests were required to deposit outside the Blue Room all coats or other voluminous garments in which weapons might be hidden. This rule upset at least one socially prominent guest, Mrs. William Sprague, who had relied on her cloak to conceal the extent of her pregnancy.

More important, four members of the Washington police force were assigned to act as bodyguards for the President. Wearing civilian clothes and carrying .38-caliber revolvers, they worked in shifts. Two were on duty from 8 a.m. to 4 p.m., another remained close to Lincoln from 4 p.m. to midnight, and a fourth was seated from midnight until 8 a.m. in the hallway outside the President's bedroom — where, one of them reported, he frequently could hear Lincoln moaning in his sleep.

Whenever Lincoln left the White House on foot, at least one of the bodyguards accompanied him, strolling at the President's side as if he were a casual companion. When traveling by carriage, Lincoln usually was escorted by a detachment of cavalry. Since early in 1864 this duty had fallen to a company of Ohio cavalry, the Union Light Guard, whose members were mounted on elegant black horses.

The Ohioans took up their assignment in time to frustrate yet another plot against Lincoln. From the first days of the War, a Southern signal officer and spy named Thomas Nelson Conrad had been flitting in and out of Washington, gathering information and passing it on to Richmond. As hopes of a Confederate victory dimmed, Conrad, by his own account, hatched a plan to kidnap the President, spirit him away to the Confederate capital and there hold him hostage.

Enlisting three accomplices, Conrad once more managed to enter Washington in the late summer of 1864. He knew that Lincoln and his family generally spent the steamy summer nights on the cool, leafy grounds of the Soldiers' Home, where a stone cottage was maintained for their use. Conrad, as he later admitted, "set to work at once to learn at what hour of the day" the Lincolns customarily left the White House, what route the President "was driven going and coming, who accompanied him, if company he had, how long he remained, and so on."

By late September, Conrad was ready to pounce upon Lincoln as he journeyed to the Soldiers' Home. His scouting led him to be-lieve that the President would at most be lightly guarded. On the evening before their "grand coup d'etat" was to take place, however, Conrad and his fellow conspirators decided to go to Lafayette Square, across Pennsylvania Avenue from the White House, and take one last look at the President as he set out from the Executive Mansion. "Imagine my astounding surprise and total collapse," Conrad declared, "when we beheld the carriage of Mr. Lincoln moving out of the grounds of the White House preceded and followed by a squad of cavalry."

The cavalry's presence caused Thomas Nelson Conrad to call off his plan. Lincoln, of course, was entirely unaware of the trouble the troopers had saved him. Indeed, the President repeatedly complained about his cavalry attendants, insisting that he and his wife "couldn't hear themselves talk" during their drives because of the clanking of sabers and the clopping of horses' hooves. Similarly, Lincoln continued to chafe about the presence of personal bodyguards. As one of the men assigned to protect the President told it: "He hated being on his guard, and the fact that it was necessary to distrust his fellow Americans saddened him." Much to the dismay of his advisers — especially Ward Hill Lamon — Lincoln occasionally slipped away from his bodyguards, visiting the War Department and other places unattended.

In December 1864, Lamon's apprehension peaked. He sat down late one night to write a scolding letter to the President, who had gone to the theater accompanied only by Massachusetts Senator Charles Sumner and a foreign diplomat. Neither of those gentlemen, Lamon protested, "could defend himself against an assault from any able-bodied woman in this city." Lamon vowed to resign

Situated on a gentle slope amid 250 wooded acres, the Soldiers' Home provided comfortable asylum for disabled veterans and men with 20 years of service. The main building (*far right*) was a residence hall, as was the cottage next door, Corn Rigs. During the summer, however, when the tree-shaded complex offered the coolest breezes in Washington, Corn Rigs was used by the President.

from his marshal's post unless Lincoln took a more serious view of his own security.

The President appreciated the concern of his well-meaning friend, but he remained convinced that he could not do his duty as President if he lived in perpetual fear, hiding himself from the people. Therein lay the seed of a catastrophe that would change the course of American history. Even as Abraham Lincoln contemplated the future of a nation finally at peace with itself, a young actor named John Wilkes Booth had already set in motion a procession of events that would lead to the assassination of the President and a wholesale shift in the country's postwar policies.

John Wilkes Booth had gravitated naturally to the acting profession. His father, Junius Brutus Booth — named for Caesar's assassin — was a British-born thespian renowned for his powerful renderings of Shakespeare's

tragedies, and for his often eccentric behavior offstage and on. Almost 25 and already recognized as a promising actor, Junius left England after abandoning his wife and small son in favor of a Covent Garden Theatre flower girl, Mary Ann Holmes. Migrating to the United States in 1821, he resumed his acting career and established his new family in the Baltimore area. He remained utterly devoted to Mary Ann — though he did not marry her until 1851, after they had produced 10 children. They settled on a spacious farm near the town of Bel Air in the Maryland countryside; John Wilkes, their ninth child, was born in 1838.

For 30 years after his arrival in the United States, Junius Booth graced and disgraced the American stage. At his best, he acted with a simplicity and a controlled power rare among performers of his time. But he tended to lose himself in his parts, to the peril of fellow actors. More than one colleague, playing the Earl of Richmond to Booth's Richard III, fled the theater convinced that Junius was really trying to kill him in the course of their dueling scene. During one *Othello*, poor Desdemona had to be rescued by other cast members before Booth, playing the title role, actually suffocated her with a pillow.

Junius Booth also marred his reputation through bouts of compulsive drinking. Once, after a theater manager had locked Booth in his dressing room to prevent him from drinking before a performance, the ac-

Citizens seeking a word with the President crowd the hallway outside his White House office, hindering security. But Lincoln was determined to make himself available. "They don't want much," he said, "they get but little, and I must see them."

tor bribed a boy to bring a bottle and hold it outside the door. Junius then imbibed to his heart's content via a straw stuck through the keyhole. Another time, when he was scheduled to appear for Act V of *Hamlet,* stagehands found Booth in the rafters above the scenery, crowing like a rooster.

Audiences and even his theatrical colleagues forgave Junius Booth his aberrations, however, because while sober he was the most mesmerizing tragedian of his day. He performed season after season in the best theaters in New York, Philadelphia and other cities and provided handsomely for his family. At home he was a loving if bafflingly unpredictable father to his children, six of whom lived to maturity. A dabbler in religion, he observed some of the tenets of both the Talmud and the Koran, and he attended Roman Catholic as well as Protestant services. Booth also believed in reincarnation — that every animal was a former human with an immortal soul — and taught his children never to harm any of the wild or domesticated creatures living on the 150-acre family farm. On one notable occasion he purchased some wild pigeons that had been shot by a hunter, bought a cemetery plot and employed a Unitarian minister to conduct a funeral for the deceased birds.

Booth's agonized compassion for all forms of life sometimes took him beyond what one of his daughters called "that exquisite turning point between genius and madness." Even in calmer moments he could contrive schemes that shook his family. Once he pursued the whimsical notion of becoming the lighthouse keeper at Cape Hatteras, North Carolina — probably hoping a retreat to so remote a spot would prevent word that he had started a new family from reaching his

abandoned wife in England. It was no doubt fortunate for ships at sea that his application was rejected. As a friend commented, the authorities would have been wiser to put out the light than to leave the eccentric Booth in charge of it.

John Wilkes Booth grew up roaming the fields of the Bel Air farm — except in the winters, when the family occupied a snug two-story house in Baltimore. His frequent companion was his sister Asia, so named by their imaginative father because Asia was "that country where God first walked with man." Asia Booth later remarked on her brother John's extraordinary gentleness and

15

his love of growing, living things. He would study flowers and insects by the hour and, true to his father's teachings, he admired animals — especially horses, which he learned to ride skillfully. "Heaven and earth! how glorious it is to live!" Asia once heard him exclaim. "Don't let us be sad. Life is so short — and the world is so beautiful. Just to *breathe* is delicious."

John Wilkes's mother also remembered her youngest son's tender playfulness. Mary Ann was the stable presence in the Booth family, a private, bookish person but indulgent with those she loved. She admitted that John was her favorite child and, in her opinion, the best-looking. With dark, lustrous eyes, black hair and delicate skin, he was in fact the most striking of the Booths — and eventually became irresistibly attractive to women old and young.

But John Wilkes Booth, for all his apparent lightheartedness, was subject to fits of raw temper. He was also consumed at an early age by a desire for fame. His older brothers, Junius Brutus Jr. and Edwin, had followed their father onto the stage. Edwin — who in time became the most accomplished actor of the entire Booth clan — was being hailed, while still in his twenties, as the equal of the celebrated Junius Brutus Sr. To at least rival if not eclipse his father and brothers became for John Wilkes a passion. His dreams of renown sometimes took a morbid — and in retrospect, an ominous — turn. Chatting with school chums about the Colossus of Rhodes, one of the Seven Wonders of the Ancient World, the young John Wilkes said: "Suppose that statue was now standing and I should, by some means, overthrow it. My name would descend to posterity and never be forgotten, for it would be in all the

This 1850 daguerreotype of Junius Brutus Booth reveals a permanent disfigurement. While performing in Charleston in 1838, Booth got drunk and attacked his friend Tom Flynn with a fireplace and-iron. To defend himself, Flynn hit Booth in the face, breaking the actor's nose and forever changing his profile and eloquent voice.

histories of the times, and be read thousands of years after we are dead."

In 1855, at age 17, John Wilkes Booth made his theatrical debut in *Richard III* at Baltimore's St. Charles Theatre. Alas, according to most reports, he was booed by the audience because, petrified by stage fright, he could not remember his lines. Indeed, lucid declamation was not always one of Booth's strong points. During another early performance, while playing the role of a Venetian, Booth was supposed to announce: "Madam, I am Petruchio Pandolfe." Instead, he butchered the line. "Madam," he announced, "I am Pondolfio Pet — Pedolfio Pat — Pantuchio Ped — damn it! What am I?" The audience roared with laughter. Engagingly, Booth laughed along with them.

The quality of Booth's stage voice was inconsistent. It was either lauded as "smooth,

When 18-year-old Mary Ann Holmes entrusted her future to actor Junius Booth, she could not have guessed what lay ahead. She quietly endured Booth's long absences from home, his erratic behavior and his marriage to another woman. Finally, after 30 years together, they wed in 1851, on John Wilkes's 13th birthday.

strong and forceful'' or deplored as "nasal, harsh and ill-trained.'' Whatever his oral deficiencies, Booth more than compensated for them with his boundless energy. He seldom walked onto a stage when his role allowed him to make a dramatic leaping entrance. John T. Ford, manager of Ford's Theatre in Washington, recalled that for the witches' scene in *Macbeth,* "Booth would not content himself with the usual steps to reach the stage, but had a ledge of rocks some ten or 12 feet high erected, down which he sprang on the stage.'' Like his father, John Wilkes performed dueling scenes with extraordinary gusto, so much so that he wounded himself at least twice and several times nicked his fellow actors. Booth's jumping-jack performances did not impress everyone. The Baltimore *Sun's* theater reviewer contemptuously dubbed him "the gymnastic actor.'' Another

theater professional found Booth's "heels in the air nearly as often as his head.''

Audiences, however, emphatically disagreed with the censorious critics. Having worked zealously to master his favorite parts and to improve his elocution, John Wilkes Booth soon became one of the American theater's most popular performers — especially in Richmond and other Southern cities, where he appeared beginning in 1858. His appeal was enhanced by his undeniable good looks. He stood only five feet eight inches tall, but his lithe 160-pound frame and chiseled features made him seem the ideal Shakespearian hero. He was soon being compared with his brother Edwin: A friendly critic in the Boston *Post* proclaimed that "Edwin has more poetry, John Wilkes more passion; Edwin has more melody of movement and utterance, John Wilkes more energy and animation; Edwin is more correct, John Wilkes more spontaneous.'' Some thought that John Wilkes would eventually outshine his brother. "Doubtless he would have been,'' said manager John Ford, "the greatest actor of his time had he lived.''

By the early 1860s the youngest of the acting Booths regularly drew large audiences wherever he appeared and commanded fees of $500 to $1,000 a week, princely sums for the time. Sighing ladies packed the theaters when his name appeared on the playbill; love letters flooded his mail.

Even with his dramatic and amatory successes, Booth lacked conceit and enjoyed hobnobbing not only with his theatrical peers but also with bit players, stagehands, liverymen, hotel clerks and barflies. Free with his money and uncondescending, he was always good for a round of drinks, in which he would join with a glass of his favorite brandy. His popularity with such lower-class citizens of his nighttime world would be a catalytic factor in the conspiracy to come.

Despite his accessible manner — and his illegitimate birth — John Wilkes Booth considered himself a member of one of Maryland's first families, and a Southern one at that. In the late 1850s, as scalding regional controversies signaled the approach of the Civil War, he sympathized strongly with the South — probably in part because of his professional success there. He declared that slavery was morally correct and beneficial for everyone, enslaved or free. He argued heatedly with his brother Edwin, who had Union sympathies — and took the position that the South had a right to secede from what he saw as the despotic government in Washington.

Already fervent on such questions, Booth jumped at the chance to take part in one of the most dramatic incidents that preceded the War, and to see for himself the arch-abolitionist John Brown. In November 1859, while walking to a Richmond theater where he was appearing, Booth was attracted by the sight of marching men in uniform. They were members of a volunteer militia, the Richmond Grays, and they were about to entrain for Charles Town in western Virginia. Their task: to guard against any attempt to rescue Brown, who had recently been captured at Harpers Ferry and condemned to death in Charles Town after his failure to inspire a slave uprising.

Somehow Booth borrowed a uniform and, armed with pistols and a knife, talked his way on board the militiamen's 10-coach train. Thus when John Brown was hung, John Wilkes Booth — increasingly a zealot about the Southern cause — was among the guards near the scaffold. Booth was deeply affected by his sight of the fanatic visionary. Although he loathed the abolitionist's ideals, Booth was fascinated by the old man's audacity and by his virtually singlehanded attempt to alter history. He was also impressed by Brown's courage in the face of death — as well as revolted by the execution itself.

It was the first and only time that Booth wore a military uniform — except for the cadet's outfit he had been required to wear as a youth while attending St. Timothy's Hall, a military school in Catonsville, Maryland. During the War, Booth was by any standard — including his own — a slacker. As an excuse for failing to enlist in the military service of the cause he so passionately espoused, Booth claimed that he had promised his mother he would never go to war — which may have been true. Mary Ann Booth and her youngest son were extraordinarily close, and she worried excessively about him.

Other people, however, insisted that Booth had an obsessional fear of suffering a wound that might disfigure his handsome face. Booth knew from firsthand experience the pain of being shot. He had been wounded in 1860 when a pistol owned by a theater manager had accidentally discharged, the ball hitting Booth either — accounts of the matter differ — in the side or in the thigh.

Booth seems to have somewhat assuaged his guilt over not becoming a Confederate soldier by purchasing drugs and other medical supplies and helping to smuggle them south, but by mid-1864 he was a deeply troubled man. As the War turned inexorably against the South, Booth undoubtedly suffered sharp pangs of conscience about the relatively inactive role he had played in the conflict so far. Like other Southern sympathizers — as well as many of the Lincoln Ad-

The Booths settled in rural Maryland, in a log cabin that expanded over the years to accommodate their growing family. Nine of their 10 children were born here, including John Wilkes (*inset*). About 1850, Junius Booth began work on a new brick house, and the family moved there shortly after his death in 1852. The people pictured above were the subsequent tenants of the log home.

ministration's Northern political opponents — he viewed the President as a loathsome tyrant. He believed Lincoln was bent not only on wrecking the South and its way of life, but also on extinguishing the liberties of all Americans through the suspension of habeas corpus and other wartime measures. Given the actor's growing sense of despair, it was perhaps inevitable that he should turn again to his childhood fantasy: making a place for himself in history by toppling a colossus.

Booth's original plan was inadvertently inspired by the Federal government. Secretary of War Stanton and Ulysses S. Grant, newly appointed chief of all the Union armies, had realized that the North's large manpower pool gave it an insuperable advantage over the Confederacy in a contest of attrition; they therefore had decided in mid-1864 to stop exchanging prisoners of war. At that time roughly 50,000 Southerners were held captive by the Federals. Before the year's campaigning ended there would be thousands more, all desperately needed to fill the depleted ranks of the Confederate armies.

To Booth the solution was simplicity itself, and his plan bore a startling resemblance to the plot being shaped at about the same time by Thomas Nelson Conrad. Like Conrad, Booth determined to kidnap Abraham Lincoln and carry him to Richmond. There, Booth foresaw, the President would be held hostage for the release of the Southern prisoners, who could then return to the fighting fronts.

Never a man much given to meditation, Booth almost immediately went into action. Sometime in late August or early September of 1864, he sent word to a boyhood friend, Samuel B. Arnold, asking that Arnold meet him at Barnum's Hotel in Baltimore, where Booth had a room. Arnold, the son of a Baltimore baker and confectioner, had been a schoolmate of Booth's at St. Timothy's Hall but had not seen him in years. Now almost 30, a strong, husky man with the sad eyes of a basset, Arnold had served for a time as a Confederate private. Sources disagree on whether he deserted from the army or was discharged for reasons of health. Unable to find work more to his tastes, he was unhappily doing chores on his brother's Maryland farm when he received Booth's summons.

Hardly had Sam Arnold sat down in Booth's room at Barnum's than there was a knock on the door and in came another friend from the actor's youth. This was Michael O'Laughlin, 26, a small, sprightly man who found his pleasures in hard liquor and loud clothes. Years earlier, when Junius Booth had removed his family from Bel Air to winter in Baltimore, Michael O'Laughlin had lived across the street. Like Arnold, O'Laughlin had once been a Confederate private. By the summer of 1864 he was a clerk taking orders for his brother's Baltimore feed business.

Over wine, and puffing away on cigars, the three men talked about the War. Then Booth revealed his plan, asking that Arnold and O'Laughlin assist in its execution.

It was a heady moment. Left to their own devices, Arnold and O'Laughlin would doubtless have gone through life without leaving a trace. But now, pleased that they had been remembered by their famous friend and flattered that he would trust them, they agreed to join his enterprise.

Once Arnold and O'Laughlin were enlisted, Booth went to Canada, where on October 18 he seems to have consulted several Confederate agents who were stationed in Montreal. These agents were concocting a variety of plots against the United States: One of their schemes was to burn down New York City. It is unclear what transpired between Booth and the Confederates, but he apparently told them of his kidnapping plan and they in turn gave Booth the names of Southern agents operating in Maryland. It was information the actor would shortly put to use.

Returning to the United States in late October, Booth began exploring possible routes by which he might take the captured President from Washington to Richmond. He decided to escape from the capital by way of the Navy Yard Bridge, at the foot of 11th Street. Beyond the bridge lay the peninsula of southern Maryland, a sparsely populated area of tiny towns and river inlets, which since the start of the War had provided way stations for Southern couriers and spies.

In all likelihood it was during this period that Booth recruited 22-year-old David Herold, a former Washington drugstore clerk who was then out of work. An avid fan of Booth's, Herold had first become acquainted with the actor in 1863, while Booth was appearing in one of the capital's theaters. Booth, who was always accessible to his admirers, had invited Herold backstage and later had sent him complimentary tickets.

On first impression, it was hard to see what use David Herold could possibly be to Booth's plot. He was of unprepossessing appearance with small weak eyes, a sharply hooked nose and a receding chin. A member of a respectable Maryland family that had moved to Washington before the War, he was now the only male in a household made up of his widowed mother and seven sisters, who alternately babied him or teased him unmercifully. To escape from his female-dominated existence, he frequently went bird hunting, usually journeying into southern Maryland to pursue his pastime.

Therein, to Booth, lay Herold's value. Because he knew the back roads and swampy waterways of the Maryland peninsula, Herold could, when the time came, act as a guide to the escaping conspirators.

During the late autumn, Booth made several scouting trips into southern Maryland. He posed as a prospective buyer of farm properties and horses and asked questions about roads, relay stations and ferries across the Potomac. One Sunday in November he attended Catholic services at Bryantown, about 30 miles from Washington, and there was introduced to Dr. Samuel A. Mudd, a Charles County physician of dour mien.

Mudd was 30 years old. His father had been a wealthy planter whose 100 slaves — according to the nostalgic writings of a granddaughter — had in better times "made the evenings merry with song, and with ban-

jo and violin accompaniment." During the harsh days that befell the region during the Civil War, Samuel Mudd had given up much of his medical practice to work what remained of the family farm. He also dabbled in real estate and horse trading.

John Wilkes Booth carried a letter of introduction from a Maryland man living in exile in Canada, and he used it to meet a number of Charles County citizens. Whether his encounter with Mudd was accidental or arranged is uncertain. As it was, Mudd asked Booth to stay over at his home, a gesture Mudd would regret until the day he died.

The next morning Booth and Mudd went to a neighbor's farm, where Booth purchased a dark bay horse that was blind in one eye. Back in Washington, Booth housed the horse in a rented stable at the rear of Ford's Theatre. To fix up the stable, he called upon a willing stagehand named Edman Spangler.

Years before, when Booth was still a boy, Ned Spangler had worked as a carpenter on Junius Booth's Bel Air home. Now a middle-aged widower, he had been employed backstage at Ford's since the theater's opening in August of 1863. A contemporary described him as "a chunky, light-haired, rather bloated and whisky-soaked man." Having renewed their acquaintance, Spangler and Booth were sometimes seen drinking together and, like so many others, the stagehand fell under the famous actor's spell. It is doubtful that Spangler was aware of exactly what Booth had in mind. But whatever John Wilkes Booth wanted, Ned Spangler would try to do it for him.

Either during his talks with the Confederate agents in Montreal or while on one of his trips into Maryland, Booth had heard of a will-o'-the-wisp youth named John Harrison

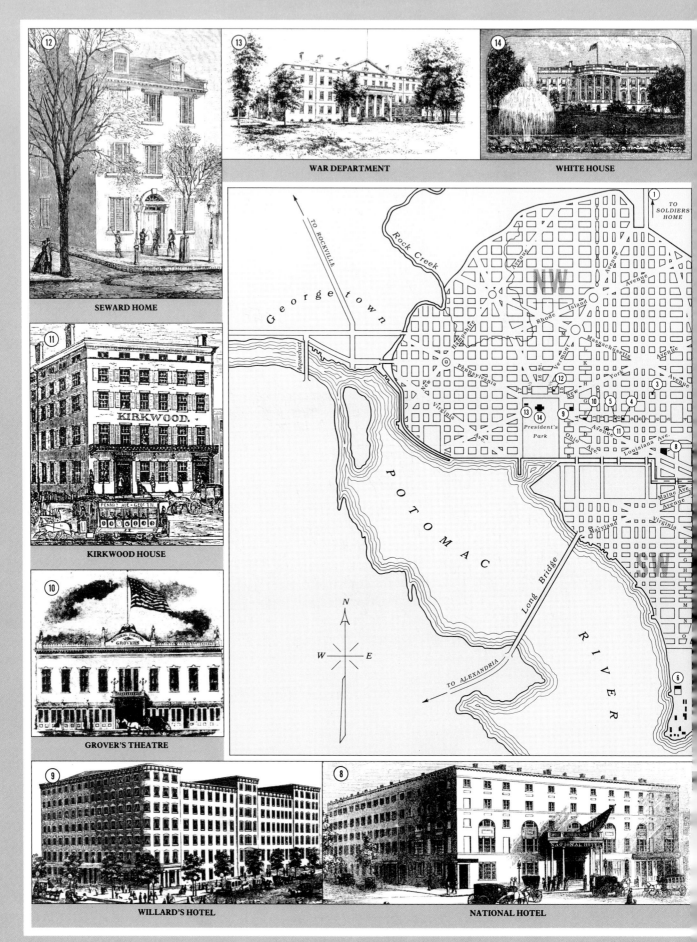

12 SEWARD HOME

13 WAR DEPARTMENT

14 WHITE HOUSE

11 KIRKWOOD HOUSE

10 GROVER'S THEATRE

9 WILLARD'S HOTEL

8 NATIONAL HOTEL

A map of Washington in 1865 is framed by pictures of places in the Union capital that figured prominently in the developing plot against Lincoln and it

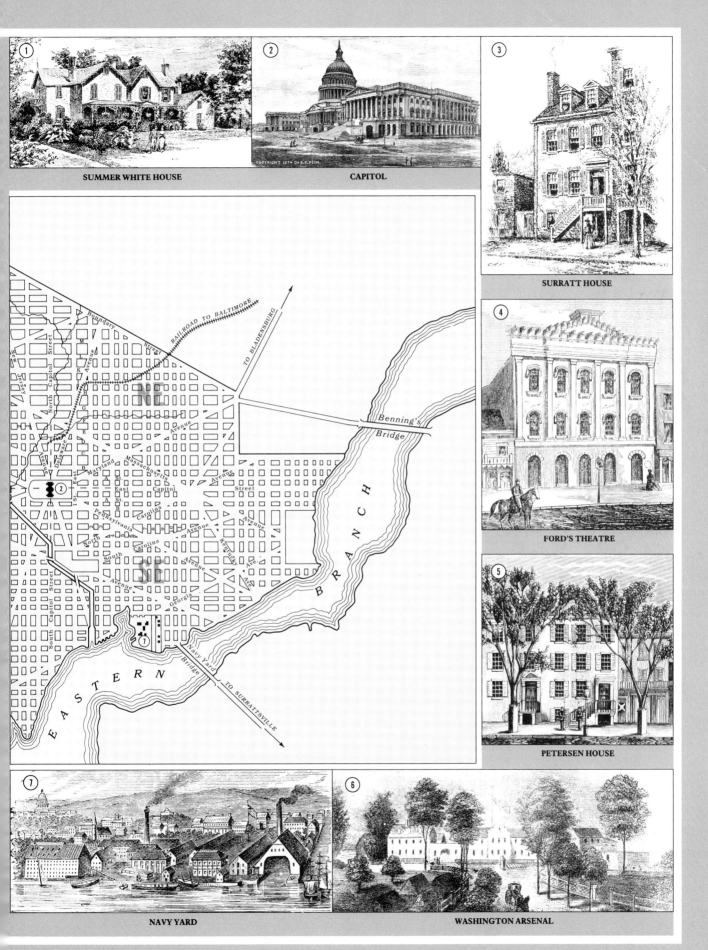

① SUMMER WHITE HOUSE

② CAPITOL

③ SURRATT HOUSE

④ FORD'S THEATRE

⑤ PETERSEN HOUSE

⑥ WASHINGTON ARSENAL

⑦ NAVY YARD

aftermath. Corresponding numbers key each building to its location on the map.

Surratt Jr. This young man, not yet turned 21, had been active for some time as a Confederate courier; he was familiar with the underground routes leading from Washington through southern Maryland to Virginia. Booth wanted to meet Surratt — and he soon got his chance.

On December 23, Booth was strolling down Pennsylvania Avenue in Washington when he met Samuel Mudd, the doctor from Bryantown. Realizing that Mudd probably knew Surratt, who came from the same section of Maryland, Booth asked the physician to set up an introduction. Booth explained, as Mudd later told it, that "he wished to obtain a knowledge of the country around Washington, in order to be able to select a good locality for a country residence."

As Booth and Mudd walked along talking, they encountered none other than John Surratt. With him was a tall, broad-shouldered young man named Louis J. Weichmann. Surratt and Weichmann had been roommates in college, and they now shared quarters in the Washington boardinghouse kept by Surratt's mother. According to Weichmann's subsequent account, Mudd introduced Booth as "Mr. Boone," and the stranger invited everyone up to his room in the National Hotel.

There Booth offered milk punches and cigars, and the four men sat around sipping and smoking. After a while, Booth and Mudd went out into the entryway to confer; then they summoned Surratt, leaving Weichmann, who had a consuming curiosity, alone and feeling left out. When they returned, Mudd apologized, explaining that he and "Mr. Boone" had been discussing a private matter. "Between you and me," he told Weichmann, "he desires to purchase my

farm but he does not wish to give me enough for it." Years later, Louis Weichmann would write resentfully that the tale about Booth as a prospective farm-buyer "was pure fiction. Nay, more, it was a falsehood, uttered purposely to deceive me."

During Booth's first meeting with John Surratt, it was his evident purpose to size up the youngster — without disclosing his developing plot against Lincoln. Clearly Surratt, a sandy-haired lad with a spacious forehead and a thin, drooping mustache, was in intelligence a cut above most of the other men Booth had gathered around him. Over the next week or so, the two got together several more times, with Booth pumping Surratt about the lay of the Maryland countryside. Before long, Surratt began to suspect that Booth, despite his declarations of devotion to the Confederacy, might well be a Federal agent. Finally, in the course of a hotel room visit, he refused to answer any more of Booth's questions.

As Surratt later told the story, Booth sat silent for a few moments; he then looked under the bed and peered into a closet, dramatically explaining: "We will have to be careful; walls have ears." Drawing a chair close to Surratt, he whispered that he planned "to kidnap President Lincoln and carry him off to Richmond."

"I confess that I stood aghast at the proposition," Surratt recalled, "and looked upon it as a foolhardy undertaking."

But Surratt — like Arnold and O'Laughlin — was strongly Southern in his sympathies. And John Wilkes Booth was nothing if not persuasive. The more Surratt considered Booth's suggestion, the better he liked it. The idea of striking such a stupendous blow for the Confederacy was tempting. Two days

Charismatic John Wilkes Booth had little trouble enlisting this eclectic band of Southern sympathizers as accomplices. Booth's boyhood friends Samuel Arnold and Michael O'Laughlin, as well as his Washington acquaintances Edman Spangler and David Herold, were easily recruited by the persuasive actor. John Surratt, a Confederate courier sought out by Booth, regarded the plan skeptically at first, but he soon joined the group and helped Booth acquire the services of riverboatman George Atzerodt.

after being told of the plot, John Surratt agreed to participate.

There was little in Surratt's background to suggest that he was a born conspirator. Until coming to the city he had lived in a minuscule crossroads community 13 miles from Washington on the Maryland peninsula, where his late father had owned some farmland and a tavern. Unfortunately, the elder Surratt had spent much of his time consuming copiously from the tavern's whiskey barrel. Because the U.S. government, overlook-

ing his drinking, had made Surratt the local postmaster, the otherwise nameless hamlet had been dubbed Surrattsville.

Upon his death in 1862 Surratt had left to his widow, Mary Elizabeth Surratt, and his three children — Isaac, a Confederate soldier; John; and daughter Anna — little but the farm and the tavern, both heavily in debt. For a while Mary Surratt continued to run the family properties herself. A buxom woman who combed her hair back into a severe bun, Mrs. Surratt peered through near-

JOHN SURRATT

DAVID HEROLD

MICHAEL O'LAUGHLIN

EDMAN SPANGLER

GEORGE ATZERODT

SAMUEL ARNOLD

The boardinghouse (*far left*) run by John Surratt's widowed mother, Mary (*top left*), became a gathering place for Booth and his fellow conspirators. Mrs. Surratt, a hospitable woman, welcomed her son's guests, especially Booth. The ladies of the house were quite taken with the charming actor, and John Surratt's sister, Anna (*bottom left*), even purchased photographs of Booth at a local gallery. Belatedly realizing the danger to which he was exposing his family, Surratt told Anna to burn the pictures, but he nevertheless continued to receive Booth in their home.

sighted eyes at a world that had by no means been kind. Married at the age of 17 to a hopeless drunk, she had struggled nevertheless to ensure that her children received a decent education. John, for one, had been a divinity student at nearby St. Charles College until summoned back to Surrattsville to replace his father as postmaster — a position he held only briefly before it was taken over by a man with strong Union credentials.

Contending all the while with the backcountry louts who frequented the tavern, Mary Surratt scrimped and saved, stalling her creditors and striving unsuccessfully to collect some debts that were owed to her — until, in the fall of 1864, she finally gave up. After leasing the Surrattsville farm and tavern to a tosspot named John M. Lloyd, a former Washington policeman, she moved to Washington and opened a boardinghouse

in a three-story, 10-room brick house at 541 H Street. Her late husband had obtained the house a decade earlier in exchange for some of the land he owned in Maryland. This respectable establishment, which Mary Surratt kept scrupulously neat, would one day be described as the nest where the egg of conspiracy was hatched.

John and Anna Surratt also left Surrattsville and took up residence with their mother. To help with the family's shaky finances, John found employment as a clerk at the Adams Express Company. Such conventional work was not, however, much to his liking. As an adventurous teenager, he had started carrying messages and performing minor errands for the Confederacy soon after the Civil War began. Adroit and elusive, he had apparently aroused no suspicions and, by early 1864, he was escorting Confederate agents through the lines and carrying important dispatches to the Confederates in Montreal.

Booth's project was precisely the sort of clandestine enterprise that Surratt enjoyed, and he quit his job in order to devote his full time to the plot. Among Surratt's first contributions was the enlistment of another recruit, a 29-year-old German immigrant named George A. Atzerodt.

It had been clear from the outset that the conspirators would need to arrange for a boat to transport the kidnapped President across the Potomac and into Virginia. For that purpose Surratt went to Port Tobacco, a river town near the shadowy inlet of Pope's Creek in southern Maryland, six or seven hours of hard riding from Washington. Port Tobacco was a favorite departure point for the little boats that glided across the Potomac carrying couriers and contraband. Atzerodt, a carriage maker by day, had frequently helped to handle the oars by night. Indeed, Surratt had availed himself of Atzerodt's services before and knew that he would be available for a fee. Now he sought out the carriage maker and easily persuaded him to go to Washington and talk terms with Booth.

In the capital Booth wined and dined Atzerodt at Gautier's, a fancy restaurant run by a French caterer, where the roughhewn tradesman must have raised more than a few eyebrows. With a low beetle brow and humped shoulders, a scruffy beard and shaggy hair that poked out from beneath a brown beaver hat, Atzerodt had a brutish, unbathed look about him. Yet in spite of his sly, fierce appearance, Atzerodt was a coward. As an acquaintance said later, "I never considered Atzerodt a courageous man, by a long streak. I have seen him in scrapes, and I have seen him get out of them very fast."

Despite Atzerodt's obvious deficiencies, Booth for some reason decided to expand his role from that of a mere ferry operator to that of a full-fledged conspirator in the plot. As for Atzerodt, he was agreeable to just about anything — as long as the price was right.

By now Booth had determined that the abduction of Abraham Lincoln would take place in one of Washington's theaters. Doubtless the idea appealed to Booth's sense of drama. But the notion also had a certain craftiness and even logic about it. The theater was where Booth worked; he knew well the location of the boxes, back corridors and behind-scenes passageways in Washington's principal playhouses. Besides, as everyone in the capital knew, the President and his wife frequently attended the theater. In fact, since the death of the Lincolns' son Willie in 1862, Mary Lincoln had turned to small theater parties instead of state dinners as a means of entertaining. On some such occasion, while the play was in progress, Booth and a fellow conspirator would accost the President in his box and hold him at gunpoint while gagging and trussing him. If the chosen theater had no back stairs, they would lower their prisoner by rope onto the stage. Then the acrobatic Booth would leap upon the boards and, with the help of other accomplices, whisk the President out of the theater and on to Richmond.

It was of course madness to think that an entire theater audience would remain quiet while the President of the United States was being subjected to this laborious process — as Booth's own associates would later complain. To carry out the scheme, Booth would need still another accomplice — someone familiar with theaters who could turn off the gas lights, plunging the place into darkness, and open the right door at the right time to aid the kidnappers in their escape.

For that role, Booth settled upon Samuel Knapp Chester, a boyhood friend from Baltimore. Chester had become a character actor and was presently employed in New York as a member of a stage company managed by Booth's brother Edwin and his brother-in-law John Sleeper Clarke. Chester's career,

as John Wilkes Booth knew, had been crowned by neither fame nor fortune, and he had a considerable stake in the continuing good will of the Booth family. Moreover, Chester had been impressed in the past by John Wilkes's boasts of successful land and oil speculations and had expressed interest in being included the next time Booth saw an opportunity to invest. Soon after Christmas

Ford's Theatre, an imposing brick structure, opened for business in August of 1863. Situated on 10th Street, six blocks from the White House, the popular theater rose above a row of small businesses — including Peter Taltavul's Star Saloon (*right*), where Booth often stopped to socialize.

of 1864, therefore, Booth went to New York, called upon Chester and suggested they adjourn to a saloon called the House of Lords.

Over drinks the two chatted casually, Booth dropping several hints about a new "speculation" in which he was involved. Yet when the eager Chester sought to learn more, Booth was reticent. After an hour Booth and Chester went to another bar, then began walking up Broadway. At this point Booth suggested they move to a less crowded street in order that they might not be overheard when he told Chester about his latest project.

On reaching Fourth Street, however, Booth remained silent — until Chester could no longer contain his curiosity. "For God's sake, Wilkes," he blurted, "speak up!"

Months later, Chester described what happened next: "He stopped and told me that he was in a large conspiracy to capture the heads of the Government, including the President, and take them to Richmond. I asked him if that was the speculation that he wished me to go into. He said it was. I told him I could not do it; that it was an impossibility; and asked him to think of my family. He said he had two or three thousand dollars that he could leave them."

Chester's fears were allayed only slightly; Booth went on to explain that the abduction would take place at Ford's Theatre in Washington. Chester's part — "a very easy affair" — would be to open the back door in response to a signal. Booth continued his attempts to recruit Chester for another half hour, as the character actor recalled, and then, meeting continued refusals, issued an ominous warning. "You will at least not betray me," Booth said; "you dare not." He added that should Chester talk, Booth would

implicate him in the plot anyhow so that he "would be hunted down through life."

Having failed to enlist Chester, Booth returned to Washington, where he approached another Baltimore-born actor, John Matthews. A bit player so down on his luck that he avoided the city's most popular hangouts for actors lest he be obligated to buy a round of drinks, Matthews might have been expected to at least humor his more successful colleague. But Matthews abruptly turned the proposition down flat — a rebuff that John Wilkes Booth would not forget. While trying and failing once more to enlist Samuel Knapp Chester, Booth mentioned Matthews' refusal. "Matthews is a coward," he said venomously, "and not fit to live."

Although angry at Matthews and Chester for their refusals to join his scheme, Booth continued to believe in his plot to kidnap the President. He had enlisted six fellow conspirators. One at least, John Surratt, seemed able and determined. Atzerodt, a boatman with experience in covert missions, would be able to get the plotters and their captive across the Potomac. Herold knew the best routes through southern Maryland. Arnold and O'Laughlin had seemed eager to shuck their humdrum lives for a glorious adventure. Ned Spangler knew Ford's Theatre like the back of his hand.

Still, as the new year began, an aura of fantasy hung over Booth's activities. There had been much scurrying about, many whispered conversations and a good deal of barroom boasting that "something big" was in the works. But it is doubtful that the accomplices — with the probable exception of Surratt — were convinced that anything would actually happen.

The Stage-Struck Booths

Junius Brutus Booth, the leading Shakespearean actor of his time, did his best to keep his children off the stage. Behind the glamor, Booth knew only too well the bone-jarring travel, the bug-ridden hotels and sleazy taverns, and the one-night stands in frigid theaters that comprised an actor's life in the mid-19th Century.

At home on his Maryland farm, Booth rarely discussed his success. Instead, he advised his six surviving children to learn a trade or a traditional profession.

But the stage held an irresistible allure for the Booth brood. They put on amateur productions of Shakespeare's plays in a backyard arbor. When their father dismantled their makeshift stage, they set up shop down in a Baltimore cellar, charging a three-cent admission fee to neighborhood children.

One by one the family gravitated toward the forbidden profession. All four sons — Junius Jr., Edwin, John Wilkes and Joseph — would try their hands at acting careers. Their sister Asia married a man of the theater. Both of Edwin's wives and all three of Junius Jr. were actresses.

Ultimately the Booths became the preeminent family on the American stage. Edwin and John Wilkes in particular rose to the rank of star, competing not only with their father's formidable reputation but with each other. Geography spurred their mutual rivalry: Edwin played mainly to Northern audiences, while John Wilkes honed his talent in the South. John "wanted to be loved of the Southern people above all things," said his sister Asia.

The brothers also developed contrasting acting styles. Edwin, encouraged by his actress-wife, Mary Devlin, adopted a cerebral, understated approach that proved perfect for his brooding portrayal of Hamlet. John Wilkes compensated for a lack of training and nuance with personal magnetism and raw energy. This potent mix soon made him a matinee idol in both North and South. Among the many fans of the gifted Booth family was President Abraham Lincoln, an avid Washington theatergoer who on at least one occasion, in November of 1863, enjoyed a performance given by John Wilkes Booth — in the drama *Marble Heart*.

Royally attired, Junius Brutus Booth plays the title role in *Richard III*. His swashbuckling version of the Shakespearean tragedy was popular with American audiences; Walt Whitman wrote admiringly that Junius could "hold the audience in an indescribable, half-delicious, half-irritating suspense."

SEVENTH SEASON — BOSTON MUSEUM — No. 29.

Tremont St., between Court & School Sts.

Museum open from 8 A.M. to 10 P.M. Exhibition Room open at 6 1-2 o'clk. Performance commencing at 7 1-2 o'clock. Admission to Museum and Entertainment, 25
Cents; Children under 12 years of age, 12 1-2 cents. A limited number of
seats may be secured during the day, at 50 cents each.

Stage Manager.......... W. H. Smith | Musical Director............T. Comer

FANCY GLASS WORKING,

by Professor CARLING, who may be seen at all hours during the day and evening manu-
facturing Birds, Animals, Ships, etc., of variegated Glass. The specimens for sale.

LAST NIGHT BUT THREE OF

MR. BOOTH'S

ENGAGEMENT.

Shakspere's Tragedy,

RICHARD THIRD

Duke of Gloster   **Mr. BOOTH**

POSITIVELY LAST TIME THIS SEASON.

TRESSEL, (his first appearance on any stage,)... **EDWIN T. BOOTH**

The Popular Farce,

SLASHER AND CRASHER.

PARTICULAR NOTICE.

A limited number of Family Slip Seats may be taken previous to the opening of the Exhibition Room, which will be retained one hour after the commencement of the Performances,
at Fifty cents each seat. The Slips not so taken will remain in common with the rest of the
seats.

Monday Evening, Sept. 10, 1849.

The performance will commence with the Overture, ZAIRA, arranged by T. Comer.

After, which will be acted (last time this season) the Tragedy,

RICHARD III

Or, The Battle of Bosworth Field.

(BY WILLIAM SHAKSPERE.)

DUKE OF GLOSTER, afterwards King.............Mr BOOTH
Tressel, (his first appearance on any stage)......**Edwin T. Booth**

King Henry 6th........Mr Whitman	Lord Mayor...............Warren
Duke of Buckingham......J. A. Smith	Sir Walter Blunt............Howe
Duke of Norfolk.........Dassett	Tyrrell....................Deering
Prince of Wales......Miss A. Phillips	Lords, Officers, Soldiers, &c., by
Duke of York...........Miss Arvila	Auxiliaries.
Earl of Richmond.....Mr W. H. Smith	Queen Elizabeth.......Miss L. Gann
Lord Stanley..............Curtis	Lady Anne..........Mrs Thoman
Earl of Oxford...........Toohey	Duchess of York........Mrs Judah
Sir William Catesby........Muzzy	Ladies...Miss Rees, Mrs H. Mestayer,
Sir Richard Ratcliffe........Aiken	Misses Simpson, Thompson, Vincent,
Lieutenant of Tower.......Williams	Mason, Whiting, Christie, etc., etc.

Hibernian Pas de Deux..........**Miss Arvila and Master Adrian**

To conclude with [1st time this season] the excellent Farce,

Slasher and Crasher

Mr Sampson Slasher - Mr Warren	John - - - - - Howe
Mr Chrtstopher Crasher - Thoman	
Mr Benjamin Blowhard - Curtis	Miss Dinah Blowhard - Mrs Judah
Lieut. Brown - J. A. Smith	Rosa - - - - Miss Phillips

TUESDAY—Shakspere's Tragedy,

OTHELLO

IAGO, (for that night only)..................Mr BOOTH

Wednesday... ...HREE POPULAR PIECES.

Omnibus... ...gton street line of Omnibusses leave the Museum every
evening... Fare 12 1-2 cents. Also Coaches for Roxbury.
...ilding, corner Tremont and Howard Streets.

When Edwin (*right*) was only
13, he went on the road to
chaperon his hard-drinking
father (*left*). Mesmerized by
the theatrical life, Edwin rejected Junius' advice to become a cabinetmaker and, at
the age of 16, launched his
career as an actor.

Upon his 1849 debut in Boston, Edwin Booth was ac-
corded billing under his father. After earning his spurs
in lesser roles, Edwin won
critical acclaim in 1851 when
his father, too ill — or too
drunk — to perform as Richard III, told Edwin to play
the role for him.

As Macbeth, at the Boston Theatre (*right*), Edwin proved too timid for leading lady Charlotte Cushman. "Remember," she goaded Edwin, "Macbeth was the great-grandfather of all the Bowery ruffians."

Wearing the crimson robes and jeweled cross of a cardinal, Edwin Booth plays one of his most popular parts — the lead in the historical drama *Richelieu*. Edwin perfected his craft during four years in the wilds of Australia and California, where appreciative goldminers often showered the stage with nuggets and coins.

Re-creating one of his father's Shakespearean roles, Edwin portrays Iago in *Othello*. Edwin's determination to escape his father's powerful shadow once produced an unintended result: After he insisted on being listed "simply as Edwin Booth," a playbill announced the engagement of Simple Edwin Booth.

BOSTON THEATRE

LESSEE AND MANAGER.............Mr WYZEMAN MARSHALL
STAGE MANAGER.............Mr J. G. HANLEY

THE
EMINENT TRAGEDIAN,
EDWIN BOOTH
WILL APPEAR IN

MACBETH

Recieved on its former representation with the most

DISTINGUISHED APPROVAL OF A LARGE AND DISCRIMINATING AUDIENCE!

THIS BEING THE
ONLY TIME

The Tragedy can be performed during the remainder of this

☞ POPULAR ARTIST'S ENGAGEMENT.

THURSDAY EVENING, NOV. 19th, 1863

SHAKSPERE'S SUBLIME TRAGEDY OF

MACBETH!

INTRODUCING ALL LOCKE'S ORIGINAL MUSIC.

MACBETH		EDWIN BOOTH
Macduff....Mr W. H. Whalley	1st Murderer......Hudson
Malcolm....N. T. Davenport	2d Murderer......Baker
Banquo......W. H. Hamblin	1st Witch......W. Scallan
King Duncan....W. H. Curtis	2d Witch......E. W. Beattie
Donalbain....Miss Florence	3d Witch......J. Biddles
Fleance......Miss Sylvester	1st Singing Witch Miss B. Grey
Rosse......Mr W. H. Danvers	2d Singing Witch Miss E. Hall
Lenox......F. O. Savage	3d Singing Witch Miss Johnson
Physician......C. M. Davis	Hecate....Mr Warren White
Seyton......W. Jeffries	1st Apparition......Richards
Bleeding Sergeant....E. Barry	2d Apparition......Miss Lees
Officer......Preston	3d Apparition..Mrs Davenport
Officer......J. Taylor	Gentlewoman....Mrs Sylvester
Macbeth	Mrs Anna Cowell

To conclude with the Amusing Afterpiece, entitled

T ON A SPREE!

....Mr W. Scallan	Waiter......Mr J. Sandford
....Mr N. T. Davenport	Policeman......F. Savage
....J. Biddles	
....E. Barry	Miss Brown......Miss Blanche Gray
....J. Richards	Mrs Stichly......Mrs Stonall
....J. Jeffries	Harriet......Miss Florence

RIDAY--BENEFIT OF EDWIN BOOTH
BRUTUS! and DON CÆSAR DE BAZAN.

EDWIN BOOTH
ATINEE!

SATURDAY AFTERNOON, NOV. 21:
Booth will also appear Saturday Night.

PRICES OF ADMISSION.

xes, Parquet and Balcony	.50 Cents
amily Circle......25 Cents	Gallery......15 Cents
rivate Boxes	6 Dollars

DOORS OPEN AT 7......TO COMMENCE AT 7 1-2 O'CLOCK.

NOTICE.—A Box in the Second Tier has been assigned for the use of Colored People, who will be admitted to that part of the Theatre only.

F. A. Searle, Printer—Journal Building—118 Washington St., Boston.

Unsatisfied with several early attempts to play the mad monarch King Lear, Edwin dropped the role from his repertory. Ten years later, Edwin again donned Lear's flowing cloak *(below)* and gave what critics considered his finest performance.

At a time when Shakespearean plays rarely ran for more than a few weeks, Edwin's introspective interpretation of Hamlet *(right)* packed a New York theater for an extraordinary 100 nights. "Between ourselves," observed John Wilkes, "he *is* Hamlet, melancholy and all."

Warned by his late father never to associate the Booth name with failure, John Wilkes billed himself as J. B. Wilkes for an 1859 performance of the historical drama *De Soto*. Within two years, however, John Wilkes's popular success enabled him to use not only the family name on playbills, but also the defiant slogan: "I am myself alone."

Dashing and debonair, John Wilkes Booth bedazzled audiences with his impulsive and fiery acting skills, which contrasted with his brother Edwin's more polished style. John Wilkes's wardrobe, befitting his matinee-idol status, was valued at more than $15,000 and included such props as a dagger with an embossed hilt *(right)*.

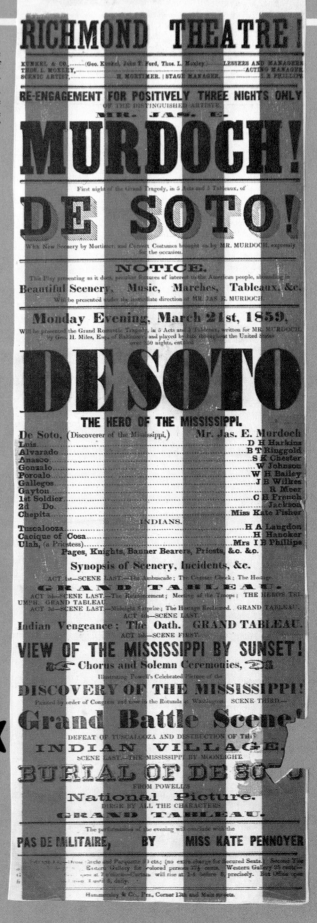

Asia Booth refused John Clarke's marriage proposals until he committed himself to a stage career. Helped by his connection to the Booth family, Clarke became a successful comedian and theatrical manager.

John Sleeper Clarke, a friend of the Booths' since boyhood, gave John Wilkes his first stage role in 1855 and married Asia Booth (*right*) in 1859.

Rejecting his father's advice to become a surgeon, Junius Brutus Booth Jr. enjoyed some stage success before settling on theater management.

Mary Devlin's impassioned portrayal of a love-struck girl, in *Romeo and Juliet*, led Edwin to abandon his vow never to marry an actress.

"Get off the stage, for God's sake," hissed Edwin to his brother Joseph (*above*) during a dismal performance. Joseph turned to medicine instead.

Australian actress Agnes Land Perry played opposite Junius Jr. during a California tour; she would later agree to become his third wife.

The colonnaded Winter Garden was the hub of the Booth enterprise: Edwin and John Sleeper Clarke leased the theater and performed there; Junius helped manage the business. The brothers' November 1864 performance was briefly interrupted by a fire next door, set by Confederate agents in a failed attempt to burn the city.

Appearing together for the first — and only — time, John Wilkes (*left*), Edwin (*center*) and Junius Booth Jr. perform *Julius Caesar* in New York's Winter Garden on November 25, 1864. Among the 3,000 spectators, each of whom paid up to five times the normal admission fee, was the brothers' proud mother, Mary Ann.

The Booths' performance of *Julius Caesar* raised $4,000 for the Shakespeare Statue Fund, a civic project to erect a likeness of the playwright in New York's Central Park. John Wilkes, who played Marc Anthony, was scheduled to return for a second benefit appearance on April 22, 1865 — one week after President Lincoln's death.

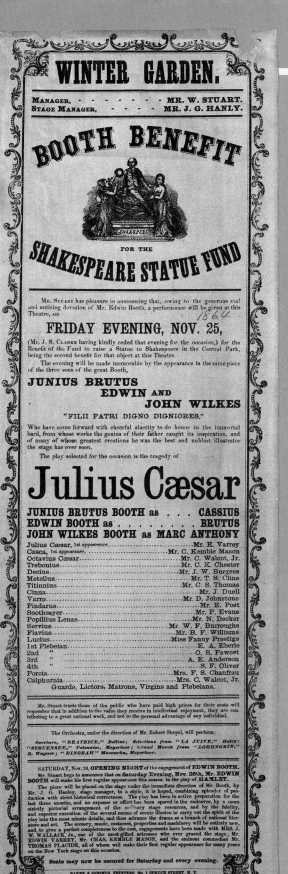

WINTER GARDEN.

MANAGER, - - - - - - - MR. W. STUART.
STAGE MANAGER, - - - - - MR. J. G. HANLY.

BOOTH BENEFIT

FOR THE
SHAKESPEARE STATUE FUND

MR. STUART has pleasure in announcing that, owing to the generous zeal and untiring devotion of Mr. Edwin Booth, a performance will be given at this Theatre, on

FRIDAY EVENING, NOV. 25,

(Mr. J. S. CLARKE having kindly ceded that evening for the occasion,) for the Benefit of the Fund to raise a Statue to Shakespeare in the Central Park, being the second benefit for that object at this Theatre.

The evening will be made memorable by the appearance in the same piece of the three sons of the great Booth,

JUNIUS BRUTUS
EDWIN AND
JOHN WILKES

"FILII PATRI DIGNO DIGNIORES,"

Who have come forward with cheerful alacrity to do honor to the immortal bard, from whose works the genius of their father caught its inspiration, and of many of whose greatest creations he was the best and noblest illustrator the stage has ever seen.

The play selected for the occasion is the tragedy of

Julius Cæsar

JUNIUS BRUTUS BOOTH as . . . CASSIUS
EDWIN BOOTH as . . . . BRUTUS
JOHN WILKES BOOTH as MARC ANTHONY

Julius Cæsar, 1st appearance	Mr. E. Varrey
Casca, 1st appearance	Mr. C. Kemble Mason
Octavius Cæsar	Mr. C. Walcot, Jr.
Trebonius	Mr. C. K. Chester
Decius	Mr. J. W. Burgess
Metellus	Mr. T. S. Cline
Titinnius	Mr. C. S. Thomas
Cinna	Mr. J. Duell
Varro	Mr. D. Johnstone
Pindarus	Mr. E. Post
Soothsayer	Mr. P. Evans
Popillius Lenas	Mr. N. Decker
Servius	Mr. W. F. Burroughs
Flavius	Mr. B. F. Williams
Lucius	Miss Fanny Prestige
1st Plebeian	E. A. Eberle
2nd "	O. S. Fawcet
3rd "	A. E. Anderson
4th "	S. F. Oliver
Porcia	Mrs. F. S. Chanfrau
Calphurnia	Mrs. C. Walcot, Jr.

Guards, Lictors, Matrons, Virgins and Plebeians.

Mr. Stuart trusts those of the public who have paid high prices for their seats will remember that in addition to the value they receive in intellectual enjoyment, they are contributing to a great national work, and not to the personal advantage of any individual.

The Orchestra, under the direction of Mr. Robert Stœpel, will perform:

Overture, "BEATRICE," Bellini; Selections from "LA JUIVE," Halevy; "STRUENSEE," Polonaise, Meyerbeer; Grand March from "LOHENGRIN," R. Wagner; "DINORAH" Mazourka, Meyerbeer.

SATURDAY, Nov. 26, OPENING NIGHT of the engagement of EDWIN BOOTH.

Mr. Stuart begs to announce that on Saturday Evening, Nov. 26th, Mr. EDWIN BOOTH will make his first regular appearance this season in the play of HAMLET.

The piece will be placed on the stage under the immediate direction of Mr. Booth, by Mr. J. G. Hanley, stage manager, in a style, it is hoped, combining splendor of production with strict historical correctness. The play has been in active preparation for the last three months, and no expense or effort has been spared in the endeavor, by a more strictly pictorial arrangement of the ordinary stage resources, and by the fidelity, and superior execution of the several means of scenic illusion to carry out the spirit of the play into the most minute details, and thus advance the drama as a branch of national literature and art. The scenery, music, costumes, properties and machinery will be entirely new, and, to give a perfect completeness to the cast, engagements have been made with MRS. J. W. WALLACK, Jr., one of the most gifted actresses who ever graced the stage; Mr. EDWIN VARREY, Mr. CHAS. KEMBLE MASON, and the eminent comedian Mr. THOMAS PLACIDE, all of whom will make their first regular appearance for many years on the New York stage on this occasion.

Seats may now be secured for Saturday and every evening.

BAKER & GODWIN, PRINTERS, No. 1 SPRUCE STREET, N. Y.

A Kidnapping Aborted

"My love (as things stand today) is for the South alone. Nor do I deem it a dishonor in attempting to make for her a prisoner of this man to whom she owes so much of misery. If success attends me, I go penniless to her side. They say that she has found that 'last ditch' which the North have so long derided, and been endeavoring to force her in, forgetting that they are our brothers, and that it is impolitic to goad an enemy to madness. Should I reach her in safety and find it true, I will proudly beg permission to triumph or die in that same 'ditch' by her side."

With those words, John Wilkes Booth concluded a letter, rambling in its content and dark in its desperation, that was intended to be his testament to humanity. At some time in November 1864, he had dropped it off, still unsigned, at the Philadelphia residence of his sister Asia and her husband, John Sleeper Clarke. Asia locked up the letter in her safe.

Since then, Booth had been a frequent visitor to Asia's home, and his behavior had become increasingly strange. He often slept on a downstairs couch, still clothed and wearing his long riding boots — the better to greet the midnight callers who sometimes sought him out. During his waking hours, Booth occasionally launched into what even the adoring Asia described as "wild tirades, which were the very fever of his distracted brain and tortured heart," against Abraham Lincoln. One night, looking especially worn and haggard, Booth murmured, "Oh, God, grant me to see the end!" — and then he burst into a song currently popular among those in both the North and the South who believed that the wartime President had assumed too much power. Each of its verses closed with the refrain: "In 1865 when Lincoln shall be king."

Early in January of the new year, Booth again arrived at his sister's house and asked that she remove the letter from the safe. He opened the envelope and at the bottom of the text wrote in large, flowing letters, "J. Wilkes Booth." Resealing the envelope, he returned it to Asia with instructions that she should open it only in the event that "something happened" to him.

The "something" that Booth anticipated may have been an imminent opportunity to abduct Lincoln. Word was circulating in Washington that on January 18 the President would attend a performance at Ford's Theatre of *Jack Cade,* a drama about a 15th-Century insurrection in England, with the veteran actor Edwin Forrest in the title role. According to at least one of his contemporaries, the information galvanized Booth. He returned to Washington from Philadelphia, determined to make a "last-ditch" effort for his beloved South, and sent word to his accomplices to join him.

How far Booth got with his plan to kidnap the President on January 18 is in doubt. In any case the exercise was futile. The appointed night proved stormy and Lincoln stayed home. Booth appears to have become fearful

ABRAHAM LINCOLN.   ANDREW JOHNSON.

PRESIDENT AND VICE-PRESIDENT.

that his machinations had been discovered, or perhaps he was merely discouraged by the winter rains, which had made the Maryland roads too muddy for a speedy escape. He put his plan on hold.

For a time the plotters went their separate ways. Booth got out of Washington entirely, spending nearly a month in New York. John Surratt used his experience as a Confederate courier to filter through the Union lines and passed some time in Richmond. David Herold lay low at home in Washington with his mother and seven sisters. George Atzerodt soaked up his lager in the dingy taverns of Port Tobacco.

Had it been left up to most of them, the conspiracy against Abraham Lincoln would then and there have ceased to exist. But Booth, increasingly agitated over the falter-

ing Confederate cause, refused to let his scheme expire. By February he was in Baltimore, trying to revive the enthusiasm of Arnold and O'Laughlin. Their specific response is unknown, but it seems likely that they once more indicated a willingness to lend Booth a hand.

The rekindled interest of Arnold and O'Laughlin — if it then existed — became less important when Booth enlisted a recruit who was potentially more useful and dangerous than Sam and Michael together. The new man was a 20-year-old former Confederate private named Lewis Thornton Powell. Whether Booth and Powell had ever met before is unknown. It may be, as Powell later asserted, that he had seen Booth perform in the theater. But at some point the two men apparently fell into conversation outside Barnum's Hotel in Baltimore and swiftly reached some sort of understanding. Booth bought Powell clothes and gave him some money; thereafter Powell displayed an unwavering devotion to Booth — whom he referred to as "Cap" — and a readiness to carry out whatever Cap might suggest.

The son of a Baptist preacher in Florida, Powell had enlisted in the Confederate Army at the age of 16 and had fought until the defeat at Gettysburg, where he was taken prisoner. In the aftermath of the bloody battle, he was assigned by his captors to help care for wounded Union soldiers. He soon escaped, however, and made his way to northern Virginia.

The next months of Powell's existence are shrouded in uncertainty. He may have enlisted for a time with Colonel John S. Mosby's Confederate guerrillas. Whatever he did from late 1863 to the end of 1864, Powell surfaced in January 1865 in Alexandria, Virginia, where he turned himself over to Federal authorities and signed an oath of allegiance to the Union. He gave his name as Lewis Paine, the alias under which he would soon become infamous.

Start Paine moved on to Baltimore and engaged a room in a boardinghouse run by a Mrs. Branson, who was thought to be a Confederate sympathizer. There Paine soon gave frightening evidence of his sometimes violent temper. Upon ordering a black girl who worked for Mrs. Branson to straighten up his room, Paine received what he considered to be an impudent answer. Thereupon, as another servant described the scene, he "threw her on the ground and stamped on her body, struck her on the forehead, and said he would kill her."

In Lewis Paine, Booth had found the perfect assistant. The young man was tall and powerfully built. He looked sufficiently respectable — despite his habit of curling his right upper lip in what appeared to be a sneer — to pass unnoticed in most gatherings. He was capable of violence, yet with Booth he was docile and obedient. And after more than two years of service with his Florida regiment, he was adept in the use of firearms. In this sense he was a true product of war, schooled in killing and apparently proud of his proficiency at it.

When Booth returned to Washington in mid-February Paine came along, and on Paine's first night in the capital he knocked on the door of Mary Surratt's boardinghouse. Answering the summons was Mrs. Surratt's ever-present boarder, government clerk Louis Weichmann. At the door Weichmann beheld a large stranger who "wore a dark felt hat, rather slouchy, and was clad in a seedy black overcoat. His two hands were buried deep in his overcoat pockets."

The visitor identified himself as "Mr. Wood" and asked for John Surratt. Told that Surratt was not in, he then requested to see Mrs. Surratt, who invited him into the parlor. There, as Weichmann would recall, Paine and Mrs. Surratt held a muted conversation, after which the landlady told Weichmann: "The gentleman would like to have some supper, and inasmuch as the dining room is disarranged, I will be very much obliged to you if you will take the meal to him in your own room." Later, in telling of the incident, Weichmann commented sanctimoniously: "Of course, I gave my permission, for I was always kind to this woman of whom I never expected any wrong."

Weichmann not only took Paine his supper but sat there staring while Paine "ate voraciously." Observed Weichmann: "He was so silent and uncommunicative. He had the eye of an eagle and was very self-possessed." Finally, Weichmann asked where his guest came from. Baltimore, replied the bull-like Paine, adding with unconscious humor that he worked in a china shop. "Nothing further was said," Weichmann wrote later, "as he continued to devour his food." Paine was given a bed in the attic, and when Weichmann arose the next morning the enigmatic stranger was gone.

With the presence in Washington of the man known as Lewis Paine, Booth's assemblage of conspirators was nearly complete. John Surratt was moving back and forth between Washington and Richmond, and Arnold and O'Laughlin were on call in Baltimore. Also waiting for a summons to action were David Herold, George Atzerodt and the befuddled but endlessly biddable handyman at Ford's Theatre, Ned Spangler. What

Confederate veteran Lewis Powell, using the alias Lewis Paine, swore allegiance to the Union in January of 1865; in March, to avoid prosecution in an assault case, he promised to stay at least 200 miles from the theater of war. Paine already had allied himself with John Wilkes Booth, however, and in a short time joined the actor in Washington.

specific use Booth would make of these men, however, was not immediately clear even to the ringleader himself.

For some of them, certainly, the work would require firearms. Booth had been collecting pistols and other weapons for several months, keeping a number in his room at the National Hotel — as a longtime actor friend named John McCullough discovered to his consternation. Barging into Booth's room without first knocking on the morning of March 4, Inauguration Day, McCullough found Booth wearing gauntlets, spurs and a military slouch hat. Before him on a table were a long, dangerous-looking knife, a pistol and a map. At the intrusion Booth leaped to his feet, snatched up the knife and lunged toward the startled McCullough.

"What's the matter with you, John?" McCullough cried. "Are you crazy?"

Booth stopped and covered his eyes with his hands; then he dropped his hands and stared at McCullough as though he was emerging from a trance.

"Why Johnnie," he asked calmly, "how are you?" Then, pretending that nothing untoward had happened, the two began to make small talk.

Whether John Wilkes Booth entertained any idea of shooting Abraham Lincoln with his pistol that day is unknown. Undoubtedly he had an excellent chance to do so. Booth had been given a special ticket to the Inauguration by a young woman named Lucy Hale, the daughter of former New Hampshire Senator John P. Hale. The Hale family stayed from time to time at the National Hotel. Evidently Lucy had met Booth in the National's public rooms and had fallen in love with him. Some who knew the couple even suspected that they were betrothed, though there is no firm evidence of that. In any event, Booth not only attended the Inauguration but also found a place on the wooden platform that had been built out from the Capitol's East Front for the occasion. Thus he was within pistol shot of Lincoln as the President gave his second inaugural address.

The speech that Booth was in such a favored position to hear was one of the most remarkable utterances in American history. Lincoln, looking gaunt and worn beyond his 56 years, nevertheless seemed buoyed by hopes for a land soon to be at peace. His eloquent address, delivered in less than five minutes from a single sheet of paper, was embued with the spirit of reconciliation. "With malice toward none," it concluded, "with charity for all; with firmness in the right, as God gives us to see the right, let us strive on to finish the work we are in; to bind up the nation's wounds; to care for him who shall have borne the battle, and for his widow, and his orphan — to do all which may achieve and cherish a just and lasting peace, among ourselves, and with all nations."

If Booth had any intention of attacking the President during the speech, it is reasonable

The National Hotel, where John Wilkes Booth always stayed when in Washington, was situated on Pennsylvania Avenue, the city's main thoroughfare and one of the few streets graced with streetlights. Just six blocks from the Capitol, the hotel had been a prewar residence for many Southern members of Congress.

to suppose that he was deterred by the rifles, in the hands of Federal soldiers, that poked from every window in both wings of the Capitol. Secretary of War Stanton, almost as concerned for the President's safety as Lincoln's friend and bodyguard Ward Hill Lamon, was taking every precaution he could. But more likely Booth attended the Inauguration out of curiosity — or to get a close look at his intended quarry.

What seems certain is that Booth would not or could not comprehend the significance of Lincoln's address. Some Southerners and Confederate sympathizers did understand that, amazingly, their archenemy — a man they had looked upon as the fiend incarnate — was prepared to become the South's best friend. With Lincoln in office the seceded states would not be treated as conquered territory but rather welcomed back into the

Union. Such thoughts did not penetrate Booth's obsessed brain. Actually, it was either at the time of the Inauguration or shortly afterward that Booth began seriously to consider the notion that murdering Lincoln, rather than abducting him, was the answer to the South's problems — or at least a proper and justified revenge. During the next several weeks Booth vacillated. For a time he reverted to his old Ford's Theatre kidnapping scheme. Then he plotted a new abduction, which would take place in less cramped and crowded circumstances. At the last he decided on a measure a good deal easier to accomplish than a kidnapping — and one far more awful in its consequences.

By the time of the Inauguration, indeed, the original reason for kidnapping Lincoln had evaporated. General Grant, confident that the Confederacy was beyond redemption and painfully aware of the deprivations suffered by Federal soldiers confined in the impoverished South, had recently revoked his order barring the exchange of prisoners. Large numbers of Confederate captives were already on their way to City Point, Virginia, where they would be turned over to their own forces. The idea of holding President Lincoln as a hostage until the Confederates were released no longer seemed to make sense — if it ever had.

The idea of abducting Lincoln nonetheless continued to have its appeal for Booth. Perhaps he thought a captive President could be used to gain concessions for the South. In any event, during the days after the Inauguration the Surratt boardinghouse became the scene of many peculiar comings and goings. Booth was frequently there, conferring with John Surratt, who was by now back from

Richmond. As Louis Weichmann remembered it, Booth and Surratt would indulge in banal conversation for 5 or 10 minutes, after which "John would tap or nudge Booth, or Booth would nudge Surratt; then they would go out of the parlor and stay upstairs for two or three hours."

David Herold also dropped by occasionally and was made welcome by Mary Surratt, whose maternal instincts were apparently aroused by the boyish Marylander. Not so the scruffy George Atzerodt, who showed up one evening and asked for lodging. He was given an attic room and allowed to stay for several nights before being sent on his way — ostensibly because young Anna Surratt had taken an instinctive dislike to him and protested that she "didn't care about having such sticks brought to the house." Regardless, Atzerodt kept dropping by to engage in whispered conversations with John Surratt and with any of the other conspirators he might happen to come upon about the premises.

One night Lewis Paine came to the lodginghouse door for the second time. Again Louis Weichmann answered. The husky guest, clad in a new gray suit and a black tie, then introduced himself by his true name. Weichmann, according to his own accounts, which were both confused and conflicting, failed to recognize the man until a lady lodger with a better memory addressed him as "Mr. Wood," the name Paine had used on his previous visit.

Paine stayed for several nights, and during that interval some odd occurrences again set Louis Weichmann aquiver with questions. Once, for example, while Weichmann was poking around the house, he opened the door to an attic room and surprised John

Surratt and Paine, who were seated on a bed surrounded by an array of brand-new spurs, bowie knives and revolvers. "The moment the door was opened," said Weichmann, "they instantly and almost unconsciously threw out their hands as if trying to conceal the articles. When they saw who it was who had entered the room they seemed to regain their equanimity."

Downstairs, in the room he shared with Surratt, Weichmann found a false mustache that had been left on a table. He assumed for some reason that it belonged to Paine: "I thought no honest person had any reason to wear one. I took it and locked it up, because I did not care to have a false moustache lying round on my table." A little later Weichmann's suspicions about the identity of the owner were confirmed when Paine came in and began looking for the mustache. "I was sitting on a chair," Weichmann noted, "and did not say anything."

On the evening of that same day, an eventful March 15, Paine and John Surratt escorted two of Mrs. Surratt's young female lodgers — Miss Honora Fitzpatrick, 19, and Miss Appolonia Dean, a nine-year-old who had been left by her parents in the landlady's care — to the Ford's Theatre performance of a play called *Jane Shore*. For the occasion the conspiratorial pair put on some airs: Surratt rented a carriage, and Paine decked himself out in a blue military cape borrowed from Weichmann. The four sat in the double box that was sometimes used by the President of the United States and his guests; they carried tickets that had been procured for them by John Wilkes Booth.

As would subsequently become clear, Booth, having revived his plan to abduct Abraham Lincoln at Ford's, had arranged

The Second Inaugural's Radiant Promise

The day of Lincoln's second inaugural — March 4, 1865 — began less than auspiciously. Through the morning hours, rain swept the city. Mud lay three inches thick on the sidewalks and 10 inches deep in the streets.

The Lincolns arrived at the Capitol separately, with a notable lack of pomp. The President had gone to the Hill early in the day to sign bills; an impatient Mary Lincoln had ordered her carriage driven around the forming procession and then on to the Capitol at a gallop.

Within the Senate chamber, Vice President-elect Andrew Johnson disgraced himself with a drunken, rambling speech before being sworn in; Lincoln murmured that "Andy" must not speak once they were outside.

The rain ended before the noon ceremony began, and the crowd outside the Capitol was surprisingly large. It greeted the President, said journalist Noah Brooks, with "a tremendous shout, prolonged and loud." Then Lincoln rose to speak, wrote Brooks, and "just at that moment the sun, obscured all day, burst forth in its unclouded meridian splendor, and flooded the spectacle with glory and with light." Lincoln delivered his brief address, which he said he expected to "wear as well as — perhaps better than — anything I have produced." After taking his oath, the President remarked to Brooks, "Did you notice that sunburst? It made my heart jump."

Dignitaries and common citizens assemble at the East Front of the Capitol to witness Lincoln's swearing-in beneath the newly erected iron dome. During his first term, Lincoln had ordered the dome completed in spite of wartime shortages; it was "a sign that we intend the Union to go on."

The magnanimous words of Lincoln's second inaugural address were swiftly reproduced in this illuminated broadside. Its vignettes (*counterclockwise from top*) depict the President, his home in Illinois, his delivery of the speech during the ceremony on March 4, and the White House.

From

Abraham Lincoln's Second Inaugural Address

March 4, 1863

...With malice toward none; with charity for all; with firmness in the right, as God gives us to see the right, let us strive on to finish the work we are in; ...to do all which may achieve and cherish a just and lasting peace among ourselves, and with all nations.

Washingtonians converge on the rain-dampened Capitol grounds to observe the reelected President taking his oath of office. In the background stands a block of attractive houses that was known as Carroll Row, where Lincoln had resided when he served as a Congressman.

Abraham Lincoln, seated at the left of the small lectern, waits to deliver his second inaugural address to an audience that included John Wilkes Booth. Some scholars of photography place Booth behind the white railing at top, just in front of the marble statue.

46

the theater party to ensure that Paine would be familiar with the theater. For a project dependent upon precise timing and swift execution, it would hardly do to have Paine blundering about the place.

At some point during the evening, a highly excited Booth appeared in the doorway of the mezzanine-level box. He asked the young women if they were enjoying the show, then summoned Paine and Surratt into the dark, narrow corridor behind the box, where the three spoke for several minutes. After the final curtain had fallen, Paine and Surratt took their guests back to the boardinghouse. From there the two men proceeded to Gautier's Restaurant for the first — and only — full-fledged conference that the conspirators would ever hold.

At Gautier's, Booth had reserved a private dining room and had arranged for plenty of whiskey, champagne, oysters and cigars. Along with Paine and Surratt, George Atzerodt and David Herold were present. So too were Michael O'Laughlin and Samuel Ar-

Lincoln greets Julia Grant while Mrs. Lincoln, Vice President Johnson (*center*) and General Grant look on, in this portrayal of Lincoln's last official function: a White House reception after his inaugural. Souvenir hunters crowded the Executive Mansion that evening and left it looking, a guard complained, "as if a regiment of Rebel troops had been quartered there, with permission to forage."

nold, called down from Baltimore by a March 13 telegram from Booth and just now confronting their prospective accomplices for the first time.

Booth, of course, presided, remaining on his feet and swigging champagne with gusto as he outlined his plot and assigned a role to each of his colluders. When next Lincoln went to Ford's Theatre, Booth and Paine would assault him in the presidential box. O'Laughlin would turn off the gas valve, plunging the theater into darkness, and Arnold, pistol in hand, would make his way to the stage and wait for the bound Lincoln to be lowered. Meanwhile, Herold would be waiting with a covered carriage in the alleyway behind the theater. Surratt and Atzerodt would be stationed beyond the Navy Yard Bridge, ready to lead the party to Port Tobacco and Atzerodt's rented boat. Once Lincoln was removed from the theater and placed in the carriage, Arnold would ride with him while Herold drove. Booth, Paine and O'Laughlin, all armed with pistols, would linger in the alley to hold off pursuers, then ride hard to catch up with the others.

His discourse done, Booth looked around for approval — and was met by an embarrassing silence. At last Sam Arnold began to speak, declaring in no uncertain terms that he wanted no part of Booth's crackpot scheme. Trying to abduct the President from a crowded theater was madness. Anyway, Arnold concluded, he was getting tired of the whole affair. If it could not be finished one way or another within a week, he intended to withdraw.

Booth doubtless was furious and some accounts have him threatening Arnold. "Any man who talks of backing out," he is supposed to have said, "ought to be shot." But Arnold and the others were seemingly unshaken by such menacing talk. Booth was forced to restrain his rage while several other conspirators voiced their objections. Even John Surratt, the practiced and elusive courier, wanted to drop the entire business. Booth heard them out in silence. Then he crashed his fist on the table. "Well, gentlemen," he cried, "if the worst comes to the worst, I shall know what to do!"

To several of the men, Booth's outburst had the sound of assassination rather than abduction, and four of them got up from their seats. "If I understand you to intimate anything more than the capture of Mr. Lincoln," one announced, "I for one will bid you goodbye." With that — as John Surratt later would describe the scene — "we all arose and commenced putting our hats on. Booth, perceiving probably that he had gone too far, asked pardon saying that he 'had drunk too much champagne.' "

So the discussion resumed. But it was evidently not until the next day that Booth came up with an alternative scheme and sought out his colleagues to explain it to them. Actors from the Ford's Theatre company, he said, sometimes gave benefit performances for convalescing Union troops at Campbell Hospital, far out on 7th Street near the Soldier's Home. President Lincoln sometimes attended these shows. Booth would ask his theatrical colleagues when the next matinee was scheduled and whether the President planned to attend. It would be a simple thing to waylay the President on the lonely stretch of road leading to the hospital.

That night Booth apparently saw some of his actor friends at Ford's Theatre and learned that some of the players were slated to appear the very next day, March 17, at

Campbell Hospital, in an afternoon performance of the play *Still Waters Run Deep*. Booth promptly passed the word, and he and his fellow conspirators began to ready themselves — unaware that Lincoln now had a cavalry escort on such outings.

According to the plan, David Herold would station himself at the Surrattsville tavern that Mary Surratt had leased to the ex-policeman John Lloyd. There Herold would collect axes that could be used to fell trees across the road to Port Tobacco, thereby impeding any Union horsemen who came in pursuit. For the same purpose, a rope would be strung across the road. Herold would also provide a monkey wrench, useful should Lincoln's carriage need repairs during its jostling, high-speed journey on the rough thoroughfares, or should it prove necessary to remove the carriage's wheels for the barge trip across the Potomac.

The rest of the conspirators, fortified with brandy, met on the gray, windy afternoon of March 17 and rode out of Washington in pairs — first Arnold and O'Laughlin, then Paine and Atzerodt, and finally Booth and Surratt. They convened in a grove of trees bordering a sharp bend in the road to the hospital. There Booth reviewed their assignments. When Lincoln's carriage appeared, Booth and Surratt would ride out and seize the reins, bringing the vehicle to a stop. Paine, following close behind them, would jump into the carriage and subdue the President. Arnold and O'Laughlin would attempt to handle any escorts Lincoln might have

Edward L. Davenport (*right*), a prominent Shakespearean actor, was accosted by his acquaintance John Wilkes Booth on March 17 outside the theater at Campbell Hospital (*opposite*). Davenport was there to give a matinee performance for convalescing Union soldiers; when he informed Booth that Lincoln was not present, Booth realized that his plan to abduct the President that day had failed.

with him. Atzerodt would tag along behind, ready to assist if needed.

Soon they heard the clip-clop of horses' hoofs. Unable to see around the bend, Booth rode out, took a quick look and signaled that an unescorted carriage was indeed approaching. Surratt joined him, and the two moved slowly down the road in the direction of the hospital, allowing the carriage to catch up and start to pass between them. As the carriage came abreast, Booth peered inside — and to his dismay saw the startled face of a smooth-shaven man who did not resemble Lincoln in any respect. Surratt later maintained that the carriage's occupant was Chief Justice Salmon P. Chase, who did attend the performance that afternoon.

Returning to the woods while the carriage continued its journey, the conspirators fell into a furious dispute. Surratt and Arnold insisted that the government had become aware of the plot and had sent out a decoy carriage to make the would-be kidnappers show their hand. They were concerned that cavalry would shortly be coming along to apprehend them.

Countering such fears, Booth argued that Lincoln was doubtless on his way to the matinee and, if the accomplices would only be patient, he could still be captured. To determine whether Lincoln was expected at the hospital, Booth rode there and encountered a longtime acquaintance, actor Edward L. Davenport, who had stepped outside to smoke a cigar during intermission. What dignitaries were attending the matinee? Booth asked him. Davenport named several, including Chief Justice Chase.

"Did the Old Man come?" Booth inquired, meaning the President.

"No," said Davenport — whereupon Booth turned to go.

"It seems to me you are in a great hurry," said Davenport.

Replied Booth: "Yes, I'm trying a new horse and he is rather restive." Then he left.

When Booth returned to his nervous knot of henchmen with this news, they scattered like flushed quail. Arnold and O'Laughlin set out for Baltimore, vowing to each other that they were through with Booth's reckless schemes. Atzerodt, after agreeing to stop at Surrattsville to tell Herold of the plot's failure, headed for Port Tobacco. The other three men rode swiftly back into Washington, arriving one after another at Mary Surratt's boardinghouse.

First to burst in the door was John Surratt. According to Louis Weichmann, Surratt brandished a small revolver and cried in great agitation, "Weichmann, my prospects are blasted; I want something to do; can you

Ward Hill Lamon (*right foreground*), friend and self-appointed bodyguard of the President, whispers a message to Lincoln during a ballet performance held at Grover's Theatre on March 21, 1865. Lamon took seriously the numerous threats made against Lincoln and warned that Lincoln's "obstinate persistency in recklessness" might cost him his life.

get me a clerkship?'' As Weichmann was attempting to calm his friend and roommate, Paine rushed into the room, his face flushed, carrying a large revolver on his hip. Then Booth arrived, holding a riding whip in his hand. As Weichmann later remembered the scene, Booth strode "excitedly around the room two or three times in a circle before he noticed me. Then he said, 'Hallo, you here? I did not see you.' "

At a signal from Booth, all three went up to an attic room, where they remained for about 30 minutes. "Then," wrote Weichmann, "they left the house without saying a word to me." The three men must have agreed it would be safer to part, at least for the moment. Booth went to New York City, and Paine, going first to Baltimore, also ended up there. Surratt, after staying at home for a few days, rode off in a buggy with a mysterious Confederate agent named Mrs. Sarah Slater. He eventually made his way to Canada, where he got in touch with the Confederate agents and saboteurs that Booth had seen the previous October. Like Arnold and O'Laughlin, John Surratt had removed himself from the conspiracy.

The conspirators could have avoided their frustration and chagrin had they noticed brief reports in two Washington newspapers that President Lincoln had changed his plans for the afternoon of March 17. He had expected to go to the matinee at the hospital. But a day or so earlier, Indiana Governor Oliver P. Morton had dropped by the White House to say that an infantry regiment from his state, the 140th, had captured a fine Confederate flag near Wilmington, North Carolina. The 140th would march down Pennsylvania Avenue to the National Hotel, where the banner would be presented to the gover-

nor with — he hoped — the President looking on. It was the sort of invitation that the politician in Lincoln could hardly resist — and so, while John Wilkes Booth and his band were lurking in the woods near the road to Campbell Hospital, Lincoln was presiding over a patriotic ceremony in front of the hotel where Booth had a room.

A few days later General Grant, judging that victory was in sight and thinking that the President might like to see the end of the Confederacy at first hand, wired Lincoln: "Can you not visit City Point for a day or two?" The President could and would. On March 23, he boarded the steamer *River Queen* for the trip to Grant's headquarters on the James River, near Petersburg. Unhappily for everyone concerned, the President's wife insisted on going along — and in so doing she indirectly had an influence on the course of future events.

In a disturbing overture to the time — still a decade in the future — when her own son Robert would have her certified as insane, Mary Todd Lincoln's behavior during the visit to City Point was at its worst. In one instance, when told by an officer that the President had given the wife of General Charles Griffin a special permit to remain at the front, the emotionally troubled First Lady flew into a tantrum.

"What do you mean by that, sir?" she inquired jealously. "Do you mean to say that she saw the President alone? Do you know that I never allow the President to see any woman alone?"

Mrs. Lincoln launched into a similar tirade upon seeing the wife of General Edward Ord riding near the President during a review of troops.

To both of those ugly incidents the commanding general's wife, Julia Dent Grant, was an embarrassed witness. Soon Julia herself became the target of Mary Lincoln's outbursts. For no apparent reason Mary cattily asked Mrs. Grant: "I suppose you think you'll get to the White House yourself, don't you?" On another occasion, when the two were together aboard a war vessel and Julia sat down on a coil of ropes, Mrs. Lincoln reprimanded her sharply: "How dare you sit in the presence of the wife of the President of the United States?"

It was hardly surprising, then, that Julia Grant had no desire for her husband or herself to be in the company of Mary Lincoln. On a forthcoming April afternoon, she would go out of her way to make sure that when Grant was asked to go along with the Lincolns to a stage performance at Ford's Theatre, he declined the invitation. Julia was not invited.

Before leaving Washington, Mrs. Lincoln had assumed that the visit to City Point would be brief. Keeping that in mind, she had extended an invitation to Massachusetts Senator Charles Sumner to come to a performance of the Italian opera *Ernani*. On March 27, an announcement appeared in the Washington *Star* that the presidential party would be in attendance at Ford's Theatre on the evening of March 29.

Booth, by then back in the capital, saw the notice and once more called together his minions — or those who were left. Paine had returned from New York and checked into Herndon House, a respectable downtown hostelry; Atzerodt had found lodging in a flophouse where men slept four or five to a room. Hoping to reenlist at least one of the

Baltimore men in his service, Booth wired O'Laughlin, telling him to come with or without Arnold. But O'Laughlin ignored the message, and Arnold had been so determined to remove himself from the conspiracy that he had agreed to go to work for a sutler at Virginia's Fort Monroe, which was held by Union forces.

No matter. Booth's penultimate plot died aborning when Lincoln lingered in Virginia. On March 29 — the date he was to attend the opera — the President was at City Point headquarters while General Grant hurled the full weight of the Army of the Potomac against the Confederate lines at Petersburg. On April 3, Lincoln exultantly wired War Secretary Stanton that Robert E. Lee's army had abandoned the Petersburg trenches. A little later came another presidential message: Richmond had fallen.

Driven by inquisitiveness and unmindful of danger, Lincoln decided to visit the captured Confederate capital. Escorted only by a dozen armed sailors and a few companions, the President walked through Richmond's downtown area to the building from which Jefferson Davis had governed the Confederacy throughout the War. The white people who saw him were glum, but none offered any threats; no rifles aimed through windows to take a shot at the tall, somber leader of the victorious Union. Regrettably, however, Lincoln's visit to Richmond may have had an unhappy bearing on the future. That he could walk unharmed through the enemy city seems to have convinced Lincoln — and some of the people responsible for his safety — that there was little danger from assassins back in Washington. Vigilance relaxed, if only slightly, at the White House, and this may have contributed to the coming tragedy.

Both Mary Todd Lincoln (*left*) of Kentucky and Julia Dent Grant (*right*) of Missouri came from socially prominent backgrounds. They had another similarity that might have made them friends: Each was raised in a family with Southern sympathies but shared the life of a man who symbolized the Union cause. Yet, largely because of Mary Lincoln's flaring temper, antipathy, not friendship, arose between the two women.

Lincoln's message announcing the fall of Richmond set off a thunderous celebration in downtown Washington. The jubilation began with the roar of cannons — 300 booming salutes to commemorate Petersburg and another 500 for Richmond — and it was still going strong on April 9, when Lincoln finally steamed back up the Potomac River. To cap it all, at 9 o'clock that evening there arrived at the War Department a telegram from General Grant that signaled the virtual end to four years of national agony. "General Lee," it said, "surrendered the Army of Northern Virginia this afternoon on terms proposed by myself."

Two nights later, with the nation's revelry still in full swing, a huge crowd gathered in front of the White House, where the Lincolns were entertaining a few friends. Brass bands blared and skyrockets roared into the night, illuminating the scene with their explosive finery. A chant of "Lincoln! Lincoln!" arose from the assembled thousands.

At length the President stepped onto a balcony above the main entrance to the White House, a candle in one hand and a sheaf of foolscap in the other. The crowd's clamor rose to such a manic pitch that one newspaper reporter, Noah Brooks, was appalled by its intensity: "There was something terrible in the enthusiasm with which the beloved Chief Magistrate was received," Brooks wrote. "Cheers upon cheers, wave after wave of applause, rolled up, the President patiently standing quiet until it was all over."

Finally Lincoln began to speak, at one point pausing to hand the candle to Brooks, and letting his manuscript flutter page by page to the balcony floor as he went along. But for most of those in the throng, the President failed to live up to the occasion. They were in a mood for raw drama — outpourings of patriotism, proclamations of victory and, not least, vows of revenge against the Confederacy that had caused so much human misery. Instead they got a long, conciliatory, carefully reasoned treatise that dwelled lengthily on the readmittance to the Union of Louisiana — where a Reconstruction government had already been installed.

One passage, however, commanded attention. Addressing himself to the question of whether the voting franchise should be extended to Negroes, Lincoln said: "I would myself prefer that it were now conferred on the very intelligent, and on those who serve our cause as soldiers."

At most that was a halfway solution, yet for at least one man in his audience, the President had just sealed his own fate. Standing beside a large tree on the White House lawn, he whispered to his strapping companion: "That is the last speech he will ever

make." Then John Wilkes Booth and Lewis Paine pushed their way through the crowd and out into the night.

These were bold words — and, it would have seemed, empty ones. Booth's grandiose plots were in tatters. Half of his band had deserted him. The Union was triumphant and, for the past several days, Booth had been drowning his despair in drink. John Deery, who kept a saloon and billiard parlor above the lobby of Grover's Theatre — and who was himself a national billiard champion — said that during this period the actor "sometimes drank at my bar as much as a quart of brandy in the space of less than two hours." Deery's conclusion: "It was more than a spree, I could see that, and yet Booth

Army wagons line up on the wharves at City Point, Virginia, to collect barrels full of salt pork and other stores that have been shipped up the James River. A mere 17 miles from Richmond, City Point was Grant's headquarters and main supply base during the final 10 months of the War.

President Lincoln holds the hand of his youngest son, Tad, and General Grant clutches his ever-present cigar in this sketch by Winslow Homer, made during Lincoln's sojourn at City Point in March of 1865. The two men understood each other, and after the visit Grant told an aide: "The President is one of the few visitors I have had who have not attempted to extract from me a knowledge of my movements, although he is the only one who has a right to know them. I think we can send him some good news in a day or two."

was not given to sprees." Just two days after Lincoln delivered his speech, however, there occurred an event that would breathe new life into Booth's schemes, sending him into a frenzy of activity.

It seemed innocuous enough at the time. On the morning of April 13, an unimpressive-looking individual in a well-worn blue uniform presented himself at the desk of Willard's Hotel and requested a suite. Once the surprised clerk had collected himself, he acceded readily, and Lieutenant General Ulysses S. Grant was soon installed with his wife and their young son in comfortable quarters.

The news spread fast in Washington, and by the time Grant emerged from the hotel a huge crowd had gathered, surging around the Union's conquering hero. A police contingent had to be summoned to convoy Grant on the short walk to the War Department, where he busied himself with paperwork. That afternoon he went to the White House to pay his respects to his Commander in Chief. During their discussion the President invited the general to join him and his wife at a theater performance the next evening.

Grant apparently temporized. He knew his wife's attitude toward Mary Todd Lincoln. Besides, both he and Julia were anxious to get on to Burlington, New Jersey, where their other children were at school. Later, when he had returned to the War Department, Grant explained his social dilemma to Secretary Stanton.

Stanton had strong opinions on the subject — as he did on almost everything. To Stanton, life was a serious matter, and he had neither the time nor the inclination for such frivolities as playgoing. Stanton himself had often turned down the President's theater invitations, and he took a perverse pride in the fact. Further, he feared that Washington still swarmed with Southern agents and that the city's public places — most certainly including its theaters — offered tempting opportunities to prospective assassins. Citing reasons of security, Stanton had frequently urged the President to stop attending the theater. He now suggested that if Grant were to turn down Lincoln's invitation, the President would perhaps be disappointed enough to stay home where he belonged.

Circulating as he did in Washington's downtown bars and hotels, John Wilkes Booth was of course among the thousands who had heard of Grant's arrival. The news set his mind to racing with a sort of crazed

clarity. He was aware, as were most Washingtonians, that Lincoln enjoyed putting famous visitors on display by taking them with him to the theater. There was no reason to believe that the President would want to depart from custom in the case of Ulysses S. Grant. The central question for Booth was: Which of the city's theaters would be honored by the presence of Abraham Lincoln and the heroic general?

Booth could see by studying the playbills that Ford's was putting on a hoary farce, *Our American Cousin*, which starred an aging actress named Laura Keene and had been around the circuit more than once. Grover's, on the other hand, was staging a brand-new play, *Alladin, or the Wonderful Lamp*. Moreover, Grover's planned a display of fireworks before the performance, along with something advertised as a "Grand Oriental Spectacle" and a reading of a patriotic poem, "The Flag of Sumter."

To Booth, Grover's seemed the best bet and he acted on the hunch. During the afternoon of April 13, he walked to Grover's and went into an office where the theater's manager, C. Dwight Hess, and the prompter were marking cue lines on a manuscript. Interrupting the two at their work, Booth asked whether Hess meant to ask President

Lincoln to the extravaganza planned for the next night. Yes, said Hess, and then as an afterthought: "That reminds me. I must send an invitation."

Booth subsequently rode around Washington, getting in contact with his remaining accomplices and telling each of them that, at last, the moment they had been waiting for was at hand. He instructed George Atzerodt in particular to check out of his low-class hotel and into Kirkwood House, where Vice President Andrew Johnson was staying. Still later Booth went back to his own room, No. 228 in the National Hotel; before retiring for the evening, he wrote a letter to his mother.

"Dearest Mother," it said, "I know you expect a letter from me, and am sure you will hardly forgive me. But indeed I have had nothing to write about." After some mild remarks about the victory fireworks displays, Booth added, "I only drop you these few lines to let you know I am well, and to say I have not heard from you. Excuse brevity; am in haste."

There was not the slightest hint of the plan now boiling in Booth's mind. Instead, it was the dutiful letter of a son to his adoring mother, to whom he had been known since babyhood as "Pet."

A Love Affair with the Camera

John Wilkes Booth, scolded a critic for Washington's *Morning Chronicle*, "has had himself daguerreotyped and photographed oftener than he has said his prayers." While Booth's praying habits remain unexplored, there is ample evidence that he was a frequent photographic subject.

Booth was a downright handsome man. His dark, heavy-lidded eyes, wavy jet-black hair and fashionable attire created such a striking image, recalled an acquaintance, that "both men and women halted in the streets and instinctively turned to admire him as he passed." Women especially were mesmerized by Booth. Clara Morris, a respected actress, wrote, "It is scarcely exaggeration to say the sex was in love with John Booth. At the theater — good heaven! as the sunflowers turn upon their stalks to follow the beloved sun, so, old or young — our faces smiling — turned to him."

To keep his image current, Booth made use of a popular photographic form, the *carte de visite*. He bestowed these inexpensive paper prints on friends and relatives and, like many other actors of the day, he handed them out at the theater.

The *cartes de visite* shown here were taken at the height of Booth's career, in the early 1860s. Booth struck a variety of poses — looking reflective and imperious in the photographs on these pages, he appears a young dandy on the next pages. One of Booth's favorites was a signed print (*below, far left*), a brooding portrait that hints at a hidden side of his nature. As Clara Morris observed, "He was so young, so bright, so gay — so kind. I could not have known him well."

The *cartes de visite* of prominent persons were avidly collected by their admirers and preserved in family albums. Pictures of the poised, self-confident actor John Wilkes Booth, such as those shown here, were prized possessions. But after President Lincoln's assassination, many photographs of Booth were defaced or destroyed — or used to make sinister new pictures. The *carte de visite* above became the basis for an artist's conception of the assassination *(right)*. In it, Booth peers into the President's theater box, clutching a pistol in one hand and a knife in the other, as a devil whispers in his ear. The montage was photographed and itself distributed as a *carte de visite*.

Tragedy at Ford's

"I must go on in the course marked out for me, for I cannot bring myself to believe that any human being lives who would do me any harm."

ABRAHAM LINCOLN, APRIL 5, 1865

It was Good Friday. Up by 7 a.m. on this April 14, the last full day of his life, President Lincoln ambled down the red-carpeted hallway from his second-floor bedroom to his office. There he handled some routine paperwork before joining Mary and their 21-year-old son, Robert, at breakfast.

Robert had just come back from the War. Throughout much of the conflict, the President had been criticized for permitting his beloved son to remain at Harvard while other young men were fighting and dying for the sake of their country. After Robert's graduation in 1864, his father tried to strike a balance between the son's entreaties to enter the Army and Mary's trepidation about his safety. He procured for him an appointment to General Grant's staff.

Now Robert excitedly told of having been on the porch outside the house at Appomattox, where Robert E. Lee had agreed to surrender his army. As a souvenir of that momentous occasion, Robert had come away with one of Lee's *cartes de visite*, which bore the general's likeness. Examining it, President Lincoln remarked: "It is a good face. It is the face of a noble, brave man. I am glad the War is over at last."

At some point, Mary Lincoln told her husband that she had obtained tickets for the new play at Grover's Theatre but had decided that she would prefer to attend the production of *Our American Cousin* at Ford's. The President replied absently that he would handle the matter.

Even as the First Family ate, bodyguard William Crook took over the day shift as Lincoln's chief protector. Crook noted that the streets outside the White House were full of disorderly men who had "too hilariously" celebrated Lee's surrender the night before, and they were celebrating still. Later he would come to feel that the hilarity had helped to create a perilous delusion: "Those about the President lost somewhat the feeling, usually present, that his life was not safe. It did not seem possible, now that the War was over, there could be danger."

About 9 o'clock, Crook apparently took up his regular station outside the President's office while Lincoln prepared to cope with the daily surge of visitors. First in to see the President was House Speaker Schuyler Colfax, who was trying to wangle himself a Cabinet job — possibly Edwin Stanton's, since the incumbent Secretary of War had already expressed a desire to return to his private law practice. It was reported that the Speaker came out of Lincoln's office looking satisfied — which may not have meant much, since Colfax's face was almost constantly fixed in the expression that had earned him the nickname "Smiler."

Another early caller was New Hampshire's John P. Hale, who had recently been defeated for reelection after 16 years in the U.S. Senate. Lincoln had appointed him to be the next ambassador to Spain. Although it was hardly the sort of thing he would have mentioned to the President, Hale looked for-

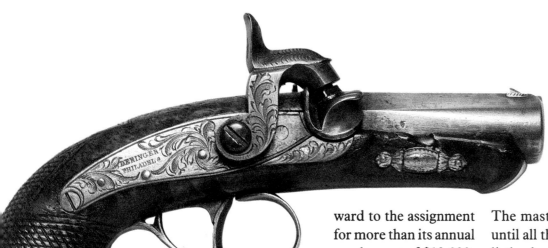

John Wilkes Booth carried this .44-caliber derringer in his pocket on the night of April 14. The six-inch-long weapon fired only a single lead ball, but Booth was confident of his marksmanship. In a Boston shooting gallery earlier that month, he had impressed onlookers by firing a pistol in a number of ways: with either hand, over each shoulder and under each arm. He hit the target every time.

ward to the assignment for more than its annual emolument of $12,000: He hoped that by taking his daughter Lucy to Spain, he could break up her romance with John Wilkes Booth. Like most actors, Booth was thought to be a notorious rake.

Coming shortly after Hale was Senator John A. J. Creswell, one of the men who had been responsible for Maryland's decision to remain in the Union. He was welcomed by Lincoln in high good humor. "Creswell, old fellow," pronounced the President, "everything is bright this morning. The War is over. It has been a tough time, but we have lived it out." Then he added somberly: "Or some of us have."

Creswell's mission was to seek the President's help in obtaining the release of a longtime friend who had traveled to the South, joined the Confederate Army and been captured by Union forces. "I know the man acted like a fool," Creswell acknowledged, "but he is my friend and a good fellow. Let him out, give him to me, and I will be responsible for him."

All too many times Abraham Lincoln had heard similar pleas. Characteristically, he let his present petitioner down as gently as possible by drawing on his immense stock of stories. While out picnicking, Lincoln said, some folks had been stranded on a river island after the boat that got them there had mysteriously disappeared. "They thought over all manner of devices for getting over the water," Lincoln continued, "but without avail. After a time one of the boys proposed that each fellow should pick up the girl he liked best and wade over with her.

The masterly proposition was carried out, until all that were left upon the island were a little short chap and a great, long, gothic-built elderly lady."

As always, the story had a point. "Now, Creswell," said Lincoln, "you are trying to leave me in the same predicament. You fellows are all getting your own friends out of this scrape, and you will succeed in carrying off one after another until nobody but Jeff Davis and myself will be left on the island, and then I won't know what to do. How should I look lugging him over? I guess the way to avoid such an embarrassing situation is to let them all out at once."

At midmorning Lincoln remembered that he had promised to go to the theater with Mary, and he dispatched a messenger to Ford's to ask that the presidential box be reserved. Apparently declining to take Grant's evasive response of the previous day as a definite no, the President sent word to the theater's management that he and Mrs. Lincoln would be accompanied by General Grant. Perhaps aware that she was not comfortable with Mrs. Lincoln, he did not include the name of Julia Dent Grant.

The main order of business for the day was an 11 a.m. Cabinet meeting, called so that the Cabinet could discuss once again the future course of the nation — and confer with General Grant. As it happened, most of the Cabinet members had gathered around the circular oak table in the President's office before Grant arrived. As soon as the victorious general walked through the door, the leaders of the Lincoln Administration applauded him warmly.

Notably absent was Secretary of State William Seward, who had recently suffered a serious accident. On April 5, Seward was driving away from his home in a carriage when the horses inexplicably bolted; the carriage went careering through the Washington streets. Desperate, Seward jumped out. He fell heavily, fracturing his jaw in two places and breaking his right arm. For the nine days since the incident, he had lain in bed wracked with agonizing pain, slipping in and out of delirium.

Foremost on the mind of everyone at the Cabinet meeting was Major General William Tecumseh Sherman, then in North Carolina and expected at any moment to announce that he had forced the surrender of Joseph Johnston's Confederate army. Although Grant, in response to questions, said he had not yet had any word from Sherman, the President seemed confident that the good news would come that day.

Throughout the War, Lincoln told his Cabinet, he had experienced a recurring dream: He found himself on board a vessel that was moving swiftly along toward an in-

At Lincoln's last Cabinet meeting on April 14, General Grant (*standing at center*) reports on the Confederate surrender at Appomattox. Shown on the far left is Secretary of War Edwin M. Stanton, and seated on the right, with arms crossed, is Secretary of State William H. Seward. Seward was in fact at home recuperating from an accident and was represented at the meeting by his son Frederick.

definite shore. In every instance, he continued, the dream had preceded some momentous event — for example, the battles of Fort Sumter, First Bull Run, Antietam, Gettysburg, Stones River. Said the President: "I had this strange dream again last night, and we shall, judging from the past, have great news very soon. I think it must be from Sherman. My thoughts are in that direction, as are most of yours."

The conversation turned to the question of what should be done with Jefferson Davis and other Confederate leaders once they were in Union hands.

"I suppose, Mr. President," said Postmaster General William Dennison, "you would not be sorry to have them escape out of the country."

Replied Lincoln: "Well, I should not be sorry to have them out of the country; but I should be for following them up pretty close, to make sure of their going."

A little later, Lincoln returned to the same subject, making it eminently clear that his policy toward the defeated Confederacy would be a merciful one. "I hope," he said, "there will be no persecution, no bloody work after the War is over. No one need expect me to take any part in hanging or killing these men, even the worst of them. Frighten them out of the country; open the gates; let down the bars." And then, fluttering his fingers as if to scatter a flock of chickens: "Shoo; scare them off; enough lives have been sacrificed."

Attention then turned to a plan for reconstructing the South, prepared at the President's request by Secretary Stanton. For the most part, the Cabinet agreed with Stanton's suggestions, which were based on the assumption that some kind of military supervision would be required to help usher the seceded states back into the Union. Even the lenient Lincoln recognized the need for troops. He hoped, however, that they would not be needed long. "We can't undertake to run state governments in all these southern states," he said. "Their people must do that — though I reckon that at first some of them may do it badly."

The session went on through the lunch hour, finally breaking up around 2 p.m. As the others left, General Grant lingered to express his regrets: He would be unable to attend the theater with the President and Mrs. Lincoln. At that moment, a messenger arrived with a note from Julia Grant. Apparently doubting that her husband would be able to refuse the President, she had written to remind him that they had to catch a late-afternoon train for New Jersey. That put an end to the matter.

John Wilkes Booth, meanwhile, had dressed carefully and breakfasted at the National Hotel, then strolled over to a barbershop near Grover's Theatre to be groomed for the most important day of his life. After barber Charles Wood had "trimmed his hair round and dressed it," Booth returned to his room, where he was visited a little after 9 a.m. by none other than Michael O'Laughlin.

Despite O'Laughlin's Southern sympathies, he had not been able to resist coming down from Baltimore to join Washington's raucous victory celebration. After a night in the capital's saloons and brothels, he had been walking with cronies along Pennsylvania Avenue when he had decided to stop in at the National Hotel and see Booth. If Booth tried during the visit to lure O'Laughlin back into the conspiracy, the effort failed:

Michael would be carousing again with friends that night, some distance from Ford's Theatre.

After O'Laughlin left, Booth launched into a round of activities that would keep him busy the whole day. First he walked to Ford's Theatre on 10th Street, between E and F Streets, which he used as a mailing address. Out in front talking to friends was 21-year-old Henry Clay Ford, brother of the theater's owner, John T. Ford, who was away visiting relatives in Richmond. Seeing Booth approach in a dark suit and light overcoat, with a black silk hat tipped on his head and a cane in his gloved hand, young Ford remarked admiringly: "Here comes the handsomest man in Washington."

In the theater office, Ford handed Booth some mail. When stage carpenter James J. Gifford came in, Ford told him that the President and Mrs. Lincoln, accompanied by General Grant, would be attending the evening performance of *Our American Cousin* and that Gifford should prepare the appropriate box for the occasion. Booth thus learned that the presidential theater party would be at Ford's, and not at Grover's as he had supposed. He apparently concealed his surprise well; he calmly opened his mail, at one point laughing at something he read in one of his letters.

Leaving Ford's, Booth walked several blocks to the livery stable where he sometimes kept the one-eyed horse he had purchased from Dr. Mudd's neighbor in Maryland. He instructed the liveryman to take the horse over to the little stable that Ned Spangler had readied in the alley behind Ford's Theatre. Because the animal was big and strong enough to carry considerable weight, Booth apparently intended that it

would be used by Lewis Paine to get away after the assassination attempt. As Booth now envisioned it, Paine's role would be to attack General Grant while Booth was attacking the President.

Next Booth walked to the stable run by James W. Pumphrey on C Street to hire a horse for himself. He got there about one in the afternoon and was shown a nervous little bay mare with black legs and a white star on her forehead. He told the liveryman to have the horse saddled and ready to go by 4 p.m. As Booth departed, he mentioned that he was on his way to Grover's Theatre, where he would write a letter.

Booth's activities for the following hour or so cannot be traced with precision — unless, it was, in fact, he who was involved in a curious incident with Julia Dent Grant. Lunching with friends at Willard's Hotel, Mrs. Grant was disturbed by the nearby presence of a hot-eyed, mustached man who glared at her so fixedly and tried so intently to overhear her conversation "as to cause us to leave the dining room." Later that same day, Julia would have reason to remember the unpleasant encounter.

At any event, it is certain that by 2:30 p.m. Booth had been to his room at the National Hotel and had changed into a riding outfit — a black suit with close-fitting trousers, calf-high boots and a new pair of spurs. Shortly thereafter, he arrived at the door of Mrs. Surratt's boardinghouse. The landlady and Louis Weichmann were just preparing to leave for Surrattsville, where Mrs. Surratt purportedly hoped to collect some money from a longtime debtor.

During his visit, Booth gave Mrs. Surratt a small package wrapped in coarse brown paper and tied with twine, which he asked

John C. Howard's public stable in downtown Washington was the site of much of the conspirators' activity. John Wilkes Booth sometimes boarded his one-eyed roan there; both John Surratt and George Atzerodt frequented the stable; and Mary Surratt hired Howard's rigs for her drives to the Maryland countryside.

her to deliver to John Lloyd at the Surratts-ville tavern. Although the package would soon assume a fatal importance in Mary Surratt's life, she almost forgot to take it along when she left the house and had to keep Weichmann waiting while she went back inside to fetch it.

After calling on Mrs. Surratt, Booth walked five blocks to Herndon House, where he found Lewis Paine lolling on the bed in his room. Apparently he brought Paine up to date on the day's developments, announced his intention of murdering President Lincoln and ordered Paine to kill Gen-

eral Grant. Paine calmly accepted the assign-ment. He ate early, and around 4 p.m. he checked out of the hotel.

Leaving Paine, Booth stopped briefly at Kirkwood House to see George Atzerodt. The clerk told him Atzerodt was out. Booth then asked for a blank card and scrawled a mysterious note: "Don't wish to disturb you. Are you at home? J. Wilkes Booth." Whom was the note for? The clerk placed it in the box of Andrew Johnson's secretary, Major William Browning, who had met Booth several times in 1864. But the note may have been meant for Johnson himself:

Perhaps intending that Atzerodt should assassinate Johnson, Booth may have been trying to determine if the Vice President was at the hotel. Whatever Booth's aim, Browning attached little importance to the brief message and put it aside.

Booth's itinerary that afternoon probably next included a stop at Ford's Theatre. Sometime between 3 and 4 o'clock, he was seen by two women, Mrs. Mary Ann Turner and Mrs. Mary Jane Anderson, who lived on Baptist Alley, the narrow passage bordering the rear of the theater. A number of small dwellings were situated on the alley, in addition to several stables, among them the one that Booth rented. When Mrs. Turner and Mrs. Anderson spotted him, Booth was standing in the theater's rear entrance, passing the time with a woman who was presumably a member of the cast. "I stood in my gate and looked right wishful at him," recalled Mrs. Anderson, in tribute to Booth's magnetic appeal.

After "a considerable while" Booth went into the theater. It seems likely that on this visit, Booth reconnoitered the presidential box. To get there, he would have had to have mounted to the dress circle — or mezzanine — and made his way around to the extreme right of the house as one faced the stage. The route would have led him directly behind the cane seats of the dress circle, exposing him to the view of anyone sitting there. Passing down the south aisle of the dress circle, he would have been confronted by a white door. This opened into a short, narrow corridor with two more doors, which were the entrances to Box Nos. 7 and 8. One fact about the three doors should have interested Booth intensely: The locks of all three were broken.

Normally, Boxes 7 and 8 were separated by a partition, which had probably been removed by the time Booth arrived at the theater in order to make a single, spacious box. From here the President and his party could look directly down on the stage, nearly 12 feet below. Indeed, if an actor were facing the audience from the front of the stage, the occupants of the presidential box would see mostly the back of his head.

Rehearsal of *Our American Cousin* had been shifted that day from morning to afternoon, and it was probably going on while Booth was in the theater. But he did not linger: He had appeared in the play numerous times and knew it by heart. When a prop-

James R. Ford, shown here with his son, was one of three brothers who operated Ford's Theatre: James was the theater's business manager, Harry Clay Ford was the treasurer, and John T. Ford was the owner and general manager. John was out of town in mid-April of 1865, leaving James and Harry in charge.

erty man he knew hailed him and suggested they go for a drink, Booth went out by the theater's stage door and had a beer in the adjoining saloon.

It was now between 4 and 5 p.m. — time for Booth to pick up the horse he had rented. At Pumphrey's, he asked a groom to shorten the stirrups; he then mounted, let the skittish animal prance and pirouette for a few moments, and rode away "sitting his horse like a centaur," as one who saw him remembered it. He reined in at Grover's Theatre and headed upstairs to Deery's Billiard Saloon, where he heartily quaffed some brandy. As he was on the way out he passed through the theater lobby, found the manager's office unoccupied and sat down to write a letter. When he was done, he placed it in an envelope addressed to the *National Intelligencer*, a prominent Washington newspaper.

Back on the street, Booth was approaching Willard's Hotel when he spotted actor John Matthews — the same man Booth had once declared "not fit to live" because he had refused to join the conspiracy against Lincoln. Now, however, Booth dismounted and cordially greeted Matthews. The two men spoke briefly about a contingent of Confederate prisoners that had just passed by. To Booth the Southern soldiers represented everything that had gone wrong with his world. "Great God," he said distractedly, "I have no longer a country."

But Booth pulled himself together and asked a favor of Matthews: Would the actor mind waiting until the next day and then delivering by hand the letter Booth had written to the *National Intelligencer*? Matthews readily agreed. As it happened, Matthews was one of the players scheduled to appear in *Our American Cousin*. He would not only

hear the pistol shot that killed Lincoln but see Booth leap from the presidential box and flee. In the following pandemonium, Matthews would return to his lodgings and read the letter Booth had given him. For reasons not entirely clear — perhaps a fear of implication in the assassination plot — he would burn the letter and not disclose its contents for two years. Matthews later remembered Booth's letter as a highly agitated exercise in self-justification, ending with the words: "Many will blame me for what I am about to do, but posterity, I am sure, will justify me." Booth had signed not only his own name but also those of Lewis Paine, George Atzerodt and David Herold.

Matthews was about to take his leave of Booth when he saw General and Mrs. Grant pass in a carriage and pointed them out. Booth immediately spurred his horse, overtaking and passing the carriage; he then turned, moving slowly by it from the opposite direction and scrutinizing its occupants. Mrs. Grant saw him and was understandably alarmed. "That is the very same man that sat next to us at lunch," she told her husband. Later, both of them would become convinced that the wild-looking stranger in the restaurant had been Booth.

As the carriage trundled down Pennsylvania Avenue, Booth rode back to Willard's and asked where the Grants were going. To the railroad depot, he was told, where they would entrain for New Jersey. Obviously Ulysses S. Grant would be absent from Ford's Theatre that night — and once again, John Wilkes Booth was forced to revise his plan of action.

Around 5 p.m., Booth reappeared in Baptist Alley. He called for Spangler to stable his mare, warning the stagehand that she had to

A notice in the afternoon newspapers on April 14 announces, inaccurately, that General Grant will accompany the Lincolns to Ford's Theatre that evening. The public report made a reluctant Lincoln feel duty-bound to attend the performance as advertised.

be secured by a strong halter because she was "a bad little bitch." He then asked Spangler and two other theater employees to join him for a drink at Taltavul's Star Saloon, next door to the theater. After gulping down his own portion, Booth told the three men to enjoy a bottle of whiskey on him — and left.

Thanks to Booth's largesse, Ford's Theatre was now empty except for the ticket man at the front entrance. And it was almost certainly then that Booth, using the stage door, reentered the theater to make his final on-the-scene preparations. Judging from circumstantial evidence gathered later, he apparently paused to pick up a pine board one and a half by three inches, which was used to support an orchestra member's music stand. Then he went upstairs and through the white door that swung inward to the little corridor outside the presidential box.

Probably using his penknife and spreading a handkerchief to catch the falling flakes of plaster, Booth whittled out a niche in the wall of the corridor. Experimenting, he satisfied himself that by jamming one end of the board into the niche and the other against the door, he could effectively prevent anyone from pushing the door open. He subsequently put the board in a dark corner, out of sight but readily available.

As stealthily as he had come, Booth left the theater, retrieved his horse and returned to the National Hotel. He quietly ate his supper and drank a liqueur in the dining room. Upstairs in his room, he put his loaded pistol —

a .44-caliber, single-shot derringer — into a pocket. Small though the weapon was, it fired a lead ball that was nearly half an inch in diameter. In the waistband of his trousers, underneath his coat, Booth thrust a sheathed hunting knife.

On his way out of the hotel, Booth stopped by the front desk to leave the key to his room. He asked the clerk if he was planning to go to Ford's Theatre that evening. When the man said no, Booth waggled a finger at him. "Ah, you should," he said. "You will see some rare fine acting."

About 8 p.m., Booth held a final meeting with his three remaining accomplices: Paine, Atzerodt and Herold. The site of the meeting is not known — it may have been Herndon House. Booth undoubtedly used the occasion to disclose the dimensions of a plot vastly more ambitious than any he had proposed before. Since General Grant had left Washington, Paine would go after another target; he would ride Booth's one-eyed horse to the home of William Seward, the invalided Secretary of State, and murder him. Herold, who had a greater familiarity with Washington than did Paine, would escort his cohort to his destination and guide him during their escape. At exactly the same time, Atzerodt would knock on the door to Andrew Johnson's hotel room and, when the Vice President answered, shoot him.

All three killings, Booth said, should take place at 10:15 p.m. Afterward the conspirators would meet at the Navy Yard Bridge,

This playbill heralds the final Washington performance of *Our American Cousin*, a British comedy featuring Laura Keene *(far right)*. An auburn-haired woman about 40 years old, the popular Miss Keene managed and starred in her own stage company, and had performed in *Our American Cousin* more than 1,000 times. Playing the title role was Harry Hawk *(below, right)*, a principal comedian in the troupe. Upon learning that the Lincolns would be attending the April 14 performance, the excited cast prepared to entertain a full house on a traditionally slow night for the theater — Good Friday.

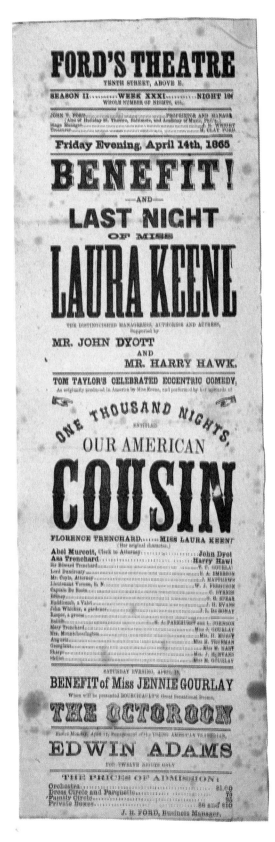

ride to Surrattsville to pick up the weapons and other items left with John Lloyd, and then gallop on to Port Tobacco, where they would cross the Potomac and reach safe haven in the South.

Of the three accomplices, only George Atzerodt had serious objections to the expanded plan. True to form, Atzerodt was both drunk and frightened. He complained that he had originally "gone into the thing" with Booth for the purpose of capturing, not killing, President Lincoln. "He told me I was a fool," Atzerodt would later testify, "that I would be hung anyhow, and that it was death for every man who backed out." The other two accomplices apparently fell in readily with Booth's new scheme. Drawing on his experience as a pharmacist's helper, David Herold offered a suggestion: Paine could easily gain entry to Seward's home by claiming to deliver a prescription from the doctor.

The meeting could have lasted no more than an hour. By the time it broke up, Abraham Lincoln had already been seated in his box at Ford's Theatre and was watching *Our American Cousin*.

After the long Cabinet session earlier in the day, Lincoln had shared a quick lunch with his wife, who reminded him that he had promised to take her for an afternoon carriage ride. Did he wish her to invite any guests? No, said the President, it should be "just ourselves."

Back in Lincoln's office, a worried Vice President Johnson was waiting. For the past six weeks — ever since his disgraceful performance at the Inauguration — Johnson had been placed in a sort of limbo, unable to gain an audience with the President and conspicuously excluded from Cabinet meetings.

Now, the two talked for 20 minutes. Although no record was kept of their conversation, it was noticed that Lincoln shook Johnson's hand warmly as they parted and addressed him as "Andy."

With Johnson gone, President Lincoln turned to some paperwork. Among other matters, he considered a plea of leniency for a Union soldier who had been sentenced to death for desertion. During the War, Lincoln had reluctantly permitted 267 men to be executed for their military derelictions. Since peace was at hand, however, he did not intend that there would be a 268th. "Well," he said, signing his name to a pardon, "I think the boy can do us more good above ground than under ground."

About that time, there was a commotion outside. A black woman had walked five miles to see the President, only to find her way barred by a soldier standing guard at the entrance. As Nancy Bushrod pleaded with the soldier to let her in, Lincoln himself appeared. Recounting the incident many years later, Mrs. Bushrod remembered the President's graciousness: He said that he had time for all who needed him and led her through the door. He quickly grasped her problem — the destitution she and her children were suffering because her soldier husband had not been receiving his pay — and he promised to do something about it. "Come this time tomorrow," he said, "and the papers will be signed and ready for you." Most wonderful of all, said Mrs. Bushrod, the President stood up and bowed to her as she left "like I was a natural-born lady."

When Assistant Secretary of War Charles A. Dana stopped by a little later, he found Lincoln with his coat off, washing his hands in a small closet attached to his office. Dana

A Lincoln Rescued by a Booth

Two members of the Lincoln and Booth families had met before the assassination, under circumstances quite different from those of April 1865. The encounter took place on a crowded train station platform in Jersey City, New Jersey, as President Lincoln's eldest son Robert (*right*) stood waiting to purchase a sleeping-car ticket for a journey to Washington. The impatient throng suddenly pressed forward, pinning young Lincoln against a railroad car. Just then the train began to move down the track, lifting Robert off his feet and dropping him into an open space between the car and the platform.

An alert bystander, seeing that the young man was in danger, dropped his valise, held his ticket in his mouth and yanked Lincoln to safety by the collar of his coat. As Robert recalled, "Upon turning to thank my rescuer I saw it was Edwin Booth, whose face was of course well known to me, and I expressed my gratitude to him, and in doing so, called him by name."

The two men did not meet again, but in the years that followed, a distraught Edwin Booth would find comfort in the knowledge that he had once saved the life of Abraham Lincoln's son.

Robert Todd Lincoln was a Harvard University student when this photograph was taken in 1862.

reported that Jacob Thompson, the Confederate commissioner in Canada who had fomented wartime disorder in the Great Lakes region, was about to take a steamer for Liverpool from Portland, Maine. Should he be arrested? Although told that Stanton had said yes, Lincoln thought a bit and then drawled: "No, I rather think not. When you have an elephant by the hind leg, and he's trying to run away, it's best to let him run."

It was time for the carriage ride. Lincoln was in high spirits, talking about the four years to come in Washington — to be followed, perhaps, by a return to his law practice in Springfield and the purchase of a prairie farm on the banks of the Sangamon River. "I never felt so happy in my life," he had told Mary. Indeed, his happiness was so marked and unusual that she felt a little taken aback and told him so. The President stroked her hand. "And well I may feel so," he said. "Mother, I consider that this day the War has come to an end. We must both be cheerful in the future."

But Mary was cautious. She replied: "Don't you remember feeling just so before our little boy died?"

By now the afternoon was waning, and still there had been no message from General Sherman in North Carolina. Accompanied by his bodyguard, William Crook, Lincoln walked over to the War Department to see if some news had happened to come in on the wire. On the way, they saw some men who had obviously been toasting the War's imminent conclusion. Abraham Lincoln had a mercurial temperament, and at the sight of the carousing men his previously high spirits seemed to disappear.

"Crook," said the President somberly, "do you know, I believe there are men who want to take my life." He hesitated, then added as if to himself: "And I have no doubt they will do it."

The morbid thought was surely still on Lincoln's mind when, after finding out that there had been no further developments on Sherman's front, he made an unusual request of Secretary Stanton. Lincoln reminded Stanton that he had a theater engagement in the evening; he then went on to say: "I have seen Eckert break five pokers, one after the other, over his arm, and I am thinking he would be the kind of man to go with me this evening. May I have him?"

Major Thomas Eckert was indeed a powerful man; although Lincoln wanted him along primarily as a companion, he might also have felt that Eckert could provide considerable protection. But Stanton strongly disapproved of Lincoln's theatergoing, and in order to discourage it he said that Eckert had important work to do. When Lincoln put the question to Eckert himself, the major confirmed what Stanton had said.

During the walk back to the White House, Lincoln spoke to Crook about his prospective theater trip: "It has been advertised that we will be there, and I cannot disappoint the people. Otherwise I would not go. I do not want to go." And when the two climbed the stairs to the White House, the President turned to Crook, who was already supposed to be off duty, and said: "Goodbye, Crook." Years later, the bodyguard would recall that "It startled me. He had never said anything but 'Goodnight, Crook' before."

Lincoln's mood improved when he found that a pair of old Illinois friends — Governor Richard Oglesby and Senator Richard Yates — had come by to say hello. Taking them into his office, Lincoln read them selected passages from the latest work of Petroleum Vesuvius Nasby, a humorist whose caustic wit particularly appealed to the President. The three men enjoyed themselves so much that Mrs. Lincoln finally had to send word that supper was waiting.

During the meal, the President tried to persuade Robert Lincoln to join them at the theater. The young officer said he was too tired. Mary Lincoln explained that she had invited a young engaged couple — 28-year-old Major Henry Reed Rathbone and 20-year-old Clara Harris, the daughter of New York Senator Ira Harris. All told, the President and Mrs. Lincoln had invited roughly a dozen people to accompany them to Ford's Theatre. Everyone but Clara Harris and Henry Rathbone had for a variety of reasons declined.

While the Lincolns were eating, William Crook was fuming. His relief as bodyguard, John F. Parker, had been scheduled to come on duty at 4 p.m. It was nearly 7 o'clock, and still Parker had not shown up. He was

The Lincolns' theater guests were a betrothed couple, Major Henry R. Rathbone and Clara H. Harris. The two wed in 1867, but their future was scarred by Rathbone's inability to forgive himself for failing to protect President Lincoln. Ultimately Rathbone's anguish drove him mad, and in 1894 he murdered Clara; he spent his remaining years in an asylum.

scarcely a dependable man: As a member of the Metropolitan Police, he had survived a long history of delinquencies and official reprimands for insubordination and drunkenness on duty. He regularly associated with prostitutes and, on one occasion, had fired a pistol through the window of a brothel. Although his spotty record was not unique among the generally lackluster wartime police, Parker had no special qualifications that merited his assignment to the detail at the White House.

Oddly enough, John Parker's position on the detail had been preserved for him less than two weeks earlier by none other than Mary Todd Lincoln. Having returned to Washington while the President stayed on at City Point, Mrs. Lincoln had taken it on herself to give Parker protection from the military draft: She proceeded to write a note certifying that he was "detailed for duty at the Executive Mansion."

On this evening, Parker reported for duty at the White House three hours late and was told to be on hand at Ford's Theatre when the President got there. The White House doorman, Thomas Pendel, who himself had once been a bodyguard for Lincoln, asked Parker whether he "had his revolver and everything all ready to protect the President in case of an assault."

Another doorman, who was named Alfonso Dunn, spoke up. "Oh, Tommy," he said, "there is no danger."

Replied Pendel: "Dunn, you don't know what might happen." And then, to Parker:

"Now you start down to the theater, to be ready when he reaches there." Shortly before 8 p.m., John Parker made his way to Ford's Theatre and awaited the arrival of the President.

Meanwhile, Lincoln was having a hard time getting away. Although his carriage was already waiting, he returned to his office to see Speaker Colfax, who had come by again, this time on routine Congressional business. Hardly was Colfax out the door when in came Massachusetts Representative George Ashmun, who had been a supporter of Lincoln throughout the Civil War. Ashmun was trying to obtain a favor for one of his friends, who was a cotton trader. When the President said something derogatory about speculators, Ashmun took the remark personally, and the President hastened to make amends. "You did not understand me, Ashmun," he said. "I did not mean what you inferred. I take it all back."

Around that time, Mary Lincoln appeared in the office doorway, attired in a low-cut, gray silk gown and impatiently pulling on her gloves. That was the President's signal: Excusing himself, he left the White House, got into his carriage and drove off into a misty night.

It was nearly 8:30 p.m. *Our American Cousin* was already well under way when the Lincolns, having stopped to pick up their guests, entered Ford's Theatre and slowly made their way to the presidential box. Young Harry Ford had personally decorated the box, flanking it with American flags and draping additional flags across the balustrade, which was dominated by an engraving of George Washington. The play came to a halt, the orchestra struck up "Hail to the Chief" and all eyes turned to the presidential party. Miss Harris took her place toward the front of the box on the far right, with Major Rathbone seated on a sofa slightly behind her. Mary Lincoln was to their left, while the President was on the extreme left, in an upholstered rocking chair that fitted neatly into the corner of the box. Although Lincoln was thus seated nearest to the audience, he was so concealed by draperies that he could be seen by those in the orchestra only when he leaned forward.

When the play resumed, actor Harry Hawk ad-libbed a line: "This reminds me of a story, as Mr. Lincoln would say." The members of the audience laughed and applauded, and Lincoln, with a smile on his face, murmured something to his wife. A little later, he noticed that Henry Rathbone was holding Clara Harris' hand. Reaching over, he covered Mary's hand with his own.

"What will Miss Harris think of me," whispered Mrs. Lincoln.

"Why," said the President, "she will think nothing about it." Later on in the evening, as if he had suddenly felt a chill, he stood and put on his overcoat. He then sat down again, absorbed in the play.

Sometime between 9:30 and 10 p.m., John Wilkes Booth rode into Baptist Alley. "Ned!" he called, repeating the summons three or four times until Spangler finally came out of the theater. Asked to hold Booth's horse, the stagehand replied that he could not stay outside the theater while the play was in progress. "But," he said, "I will call Peanut John."

Peanut John was Joseph Burroughs, who had come by his nickname selling peanuts outside Ford's Theatre when it first opened. Now he had graduated to being a general

The Trappings of a Simple Man

When Abraham Lincoln arose early on April 14 to prepare for a busy day, he dressed conservatively, as was his custom, in a white shirt and a black suit that included a vest and a long-skirted frock coat (*right*). His supple leather boots (*below*), specially made from a paper pattern of his size-14 feet, were also black and were banded at the top with maroon goatskin.

That evening, as Lincoln left for the theater, he paused long enough to gather his beaver hat (*opposite*), silver-headed ebony cane (*right*) and white kid gloves (*below, right*). The President, who eschewed any attempt at stylishness, considered the gloves a nuisance but wore them to please his wife, who felt that a gentleman should cover his hands. As soon as he was able, however, Lincoln stuffed the gloves into his pockets — where they were later found.

In the chaos that followed the attack at Ford's Theatre, Lincoln's belongings were scattered. His hat turned up at police headquarters and his cane was discovered later, still in the presidential box. Eventually, all of his possessions, including the objects (*opposite*) that he had tucked into his pockets that fateful morning, were returned to the Lincoln family.

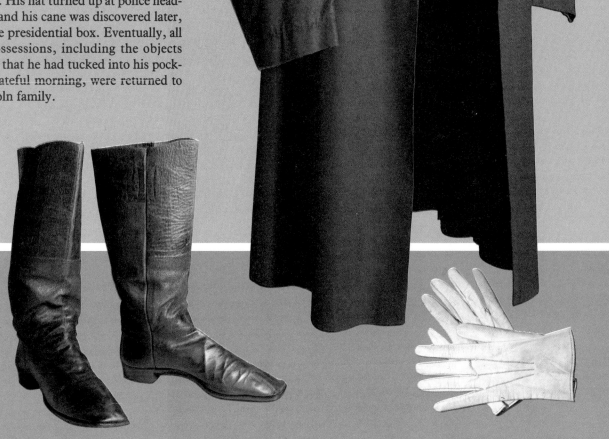

The items in Lincoln's pockets were extraordinary only for their simplicity. He carried an ivory-handled pocketknife and a neatly folded linen handkerchief with "A. Lincoln" cross-stitched in red. There were two pairs of spectacles — a pair that folded at the bridge to fit into a tiny silver case, and another set, in a leather slipcase, that had been painstakingly mended with string. Chamois pads encased in a metal frame enabled Lincoln to polish both sides of his lenses at once. The President's silk-lined leather wallet had separate compartments for currency and for notes; a small pencil was tucked handily inside the latter. The currency section held only a Confederate five-dollar bill, probably a memento of his recent visit to Richmond. Two other items shown here that Lincoln is believed to have with him that night were a pyramid-shaped watch fob of gold-bearing quartz, and an enamel cuff button bearing the gold initial "L." The button may have popped off Lincoln's shirt as doctors examined him.

handyman. That afternoon, as it happened, he had exchanged harsh words with Spangler while the two of them prepared the presidential box. Spangler had cursed Lincoln, and Peanut John had protested: "What do you want to damn him for? He never did anything to you."

The stagehand had answered: "Aw, he ought to be shot for getting all those men killed in the War."

Tonight, however, Peanut John seemed happy enough to do as Spangler wished. Taking the reins of Booth's little mare, he settled down on a bench in Baptist Alley to await the actor's return.

Inside Ford's, Booth asked if he could cross the stage behind the scenery. No, a worker told him, because the scene then being played occupied the entire stage. Instead, Booth took a route beneath the stage and went out a side door into a passageway that led toward the front of the theater and Taltavul's saloon.

Booth turned into the saloon, ordered whiskey and chased it with water. A drunk at the bar recognized him. "You'll never be the actor your father was," he told Booth. These would have been fighting words in the past — but Booth only smiled. "When I leave the stage," he said, "I will be the most famous man in America."

From Taltavul's, Booth walked the few steps to the front of the theater, restlessly ducking in and out of the playhouse at least five times. Finally he approached the doorkeeper, John E. Buckingham, asking him for a chew of tobacco and also for the time. Buckingham reminded him that there was a clock in the lobby.

It was a little after 10 p.m. Booth walked through the lobby and up the stairs to the dress circle. There he paused and looked around as if counting the house. Several in the audience noticed and recognized him as he turned and made his way toward the white door leading to the corridor outside the presidential box.

Army Captain Theodore McGowan, who was close by, testified later that Booth took a pack of visiting cards from his pocket. The actor showed one of them to the President's footman and messenger, Charles Forbes, who was sitting near the white door. Then John Wilkes Booth went inside and closed the door behind him.

And where was John Parker, the bodyguard who was responsible for ensuring the safety of Abraham Lincoln?

After ushering the presidential party into their theater box, Parker had presumably seated himself outside the white door, where he could see very little of the action on the stage. Given his character, he may have been tempted to desert his post and find a better seat from which to watch the play. That, at least, was the opinion of his fellow bodyguard, William Crook. In reminiscences published nearly half a century after the event, Crook claimed that Parker had confessed to him the day after the assassination that he had moved to a seat at the front of the dress circle. A more contemporary account was given by Lincoln's coachman, Francis Burns, who testified during the trial of the conspirators that, at one point in the evening, Parker had gone with him and Charles Forbes to have a drink at Taltavul's Star Saloon.

On the other hand, charges of "neglect of duty" later brought against Parker were dismissed. He continued to serve on the White

The seat Abraham Lincoln occupied at Ford's Theatre was this tufted walnut rocking chair, which Harry Ford had removed from his personal quarters and placed in the presidential box. A sofa and chairs, each covered in crimson velvet, completed the furnishings of the box.

House detail for a month after the assassination and on the police force itself for another three years. Exactly why he was exonerated is unclear to this day — the trial board records have never been found — but it is possible that his instructions were simply to get the President safely into the theater and not to guard the presidential box. It is also conceivable that Lincoln dismissed Parker and told him to enjoy watching the play; such a gesture would have been completely in character for the President.

In any event, Parker was not seen again until 6 o'clock the following morning, when he appeared at a police station with an inebriated prostitute, Lizzie Williams, in tow. Parker wanted to have the prostitute booked, but the police were far too busy at that point to bother themselves with the likes of Lizzie Williams. The desk officer released her — and suggested to John Parker, who seemed to be tired, that he had better go home and try to get some sleep.

Whatever the bodyguard's real story may have been, the way to the presidential box lay open to John Wilkes Booth. He made the most of his chance.

Moving swiftly, Booth slipped into the corridor outside the box, picked up the pine board he had hidden earlier, and jammed it into the angle between the closed door and the wall. He may very well have stopped to peer through a small hole that had been drilled by the theater management in the door of Box 7. Its purpose was to provide the guard with a means of observing the presidential party during a performance without disturbing them in any way.

Onstage, *Our American Cousin* was nearing a moment of merriment. An avaricious English dowager named Mrs. Mountchessington, believing that Asa Trenchard — the cousin of the title role — was an American millionaire, had been trying to land him for her daughter. Mrs. Mountchessington had just discovered, however, that Trenchard was in reality nothing more than a country bumpkin and far from rich.

Down in the audience, a young woman named Julia Adelaide Shephard was scribbling a note to her father back home even as she watched the play. "The President," she wrote, "is in yonder upper right hand private box. The young and lovely daughter of Senator Harris is the only one of the party we can see, as the flags hide the rest. But we know 'Father Abraham' is there, like a father watching what interests his children. How sociable it seems, like one family sitting around their parlor fire." She described a little of the plot and added: "We are waiting for the next scene."

She heard the furious Mrs. Mountchessington take out her frustration on Trenchard: "I am aware, Mr. Trenchard, that you are not used to the manners of polite society." As actress Laura Keene swept offstage, the audience got ready for the laugh

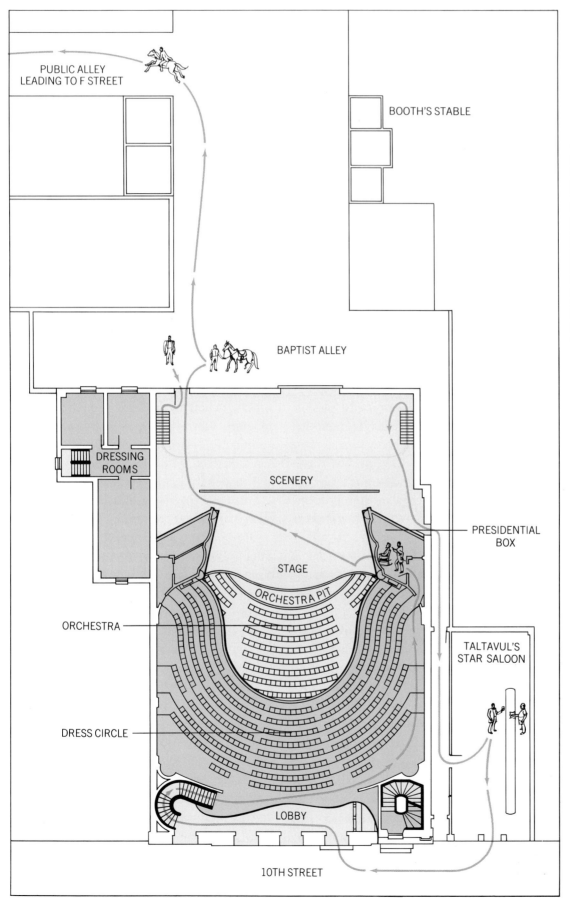

PUBLIC ALLEY
LEADING TO F STREET

BOOTH'S STABLE

BAPTIST ALLEY

DRESSING
ROOMS

SCENERY

PRESIDENTIAL
BOX

STAGE

ORCHESTRA PIT

ORCHESTRA

TALTAVUL'S
STAR SALOON

DRESS CIRCLE

LOBBY

10TH STREET

The diagram at left — depicting the first and second levels of Ford's Theatre, its outbuildings and the saloon next door — traces the route of John Wilkes Booth as he assassinated President Lincoln and then escaped across the stage and down a back alley. Booth reached the presidential box, located on the theater's second level, by climbing the stairs from the lobby and crossing to the opposite side of the dress circle. There a door opened into a narrow vestibule, from which the box — actually two small boxes combined to make a single, large one — could be entered through either of two doors (*right*).

they knew was coming. Harry Hawk, playing the role of Trenchard, gave it to them: "Heh, heh. Don't know the manners of good society, eh? Well, I guess I know enough to turn you inside out, old gal — you sockdologizing old man-trap."

As laughter filled Ford's Theatre, John Wilkes Booth slipped into the presidential box and approached the presidential rocking chair from the right side. There was a witness to his arrival: On the opposite side of the theater sat a restaurant owner named James P. Ferguson, who had come to Ford's Theatre that night in the hope of seeing his idol, General Grant. Ferguson was watching the box intently, trying to make out if the shadowy figure that had entered was indeed Grant, arriving late. The President was leaning forward with his hand on the railing, looking down at someone in the orchestra. Suddenly he turned his head sharply to the left — perhaps because he had glimpsed the pistol pointed at the back right side of his head and was trying instinctively to shy away. An instant later, Ferguson saw the flash of Booth's derringer. The audience was still laughing when Booth's single shot hit Lincoln behind the left ear and tore into his brain. The President reflexively threw up his right hand; then, as if nodding off to sleep, he slumped in his rocker. Next to him, Mary Lincoln had heard the shot. Looking at her husband, she saw him beginning to sag. She reached over to brace him.

Major Henry Rathbone had heard the shot too. He looked around and through the smoke saw Booth. The assassin shouted a word that sounded like "Freedom!" and Rathbone lunged toward him. Dropping his empty pistol, Booth drew his knife and slashed at his assailant. To parry the blow, Rathbone raised his left arm and was gashed to the bone. Again he grappled with the assassin. Breaking loose, Booth climbed onto the railing of the box and leaped the 12 feet to the stage. His right spur caught in one of the decorative flags, causing him to land off-balance, with the weight of his entire body concentrated on his left foot.

The shock of impact broke the fibula, the smaller of the two bones in Booth's lower left leg. He was able to get to his feet and hobble — if he had broken the larger tibia he would have been unable to walk at all — but he was in agonizing pain. Nevertheless, he brandished his knife, snarled *"Sic semper tyrannis!"* ("Thus always to tyrants") and escaped across the stage in what one witness described as a kind of bullfrog hop. Only Harry Hawk impeded his ungainly progress, and Hawk, unarmed, did the sensible thing — he turned and ran. Not until he had clambered up a flight of stairs did the comedian stop and say to himself: "My God, that's John Booth!"

Scarcely more than 30 seconds had elapsed from the time Booth entered the presidential box until he leaped to the stage and fled. The more than 1,000 people in the house were only now beginning to stir. Amid the laughter, many had not heard the shot at all. Those who had, looked up to see nothing but a wisp of smoke curling from the presidential box: Lincoln himself was out of sight, still hidden by draperies. Even when a wild-eyed man dropped to the stage, some of the spectators assumed he was part of the act and continued to laugh. Then they heard Major Rathbone's shouts of "Stop that man!" and the screams of Mary Lincoln.

Two men recovered themselves faster than the others. One was A. C. Richards, superintendent of the Metropolitan Police, who was sitting in the dress circle. When he saw Booth limp away, Richards rushed down the stairs and bounded onto the stage. Already there was Joseph B. Stewart, a Washington lawyer who had been sitting in an orchestra seat. Together the two men searched the scenery and the shadowy backstage area.

Booth, meantime, had scuttled to the wing at the left of the stage, knife still in hand. Laura Keene was there waiting for her cue. Booth knocked her aside and plunged down the passageway leading to the rear exit. In his way stood William Withers Jr., the theater's orchestra leader, who had gone backstage during a break. Booth's knife flashed twice, once ripping clothing and then opening a wound in the back of the musician's neck. Withers fell to the floor. Booth moved past him and out the door.

In the alley, Peanut John had just got up from his bench, still holding Booth's horse. Booth hopped from the theater and started to mount, demanding the reins. Evidently the youth moved too slowly: Booth knocked him down with the butt end of his knife and kicked him. Then he pulled himself into the saddle and galloped away.

Peanut John was back on his feet by the time Richards and Stewart had located the rear door and stepped out into Baptist Alley. As they questioned the stagehand — who claimed he had been holding a horse for a man he did not know — they could hear a horse galloping away at the end of the alley. John Wilkes Booth had escaped from the scene of his crime.

By now everyone in Ford's Theatre knew what had happened. One member of the play's cast would forever remember "the shouts, groans, curses, smashing of seats, screams of women, cries of terror." Many people were in tears. Upstairs in the dress circle, seated within 40 feet of the presidential box, was a 23-year-old surgeon named Charles A. Leale. As it happened, Dr. Leale was employed in an army hospital and was familiar with gunshot wounds. Shoving his way through the milling crowd, Leale made his way to the white door outside the presidential box just as Major Rathbone was removing the board that Booth had used to jam it shut. Leale looked for a moment at Rathbone's injury; he then went quickly into the presidential box.

There, in his rocking chair, sat Abraham Lincoln, eyes closed, head dropping forward, chin on chest. Mary Lincoln was bending over the President, attempting to hold him upright. "Oh, doctor," she cried, "what can you do for my poor husband? Is he dead? Can he recover?"

To Leale, Lincoln appeared dead. "I placed my finger on the President's right radial pulse," he said later, "but could perceive no movement of the artery." Having recognized Rathbone's injury as a knife wound, Leale assumed that the President had also been stabbed. With help from others in the box, he removed Lincoln from the chair and laid him out on the floor. When the President's upper clothing was cut away, however, Leale could find no wound. It was only then that he lifted the eyelids and saw evidence of brain injury. Passing his fingers through Lincoln's blood-matted hair, Leale found a half-inch hole in the back of the skull. He quickly probed with the little finger of his left hand and removed a clot, thereby opening the wound and relieving pressure on the brain.

In the aftermath of the assassination, contemporary artists rushed to draw their perceptions of the tragic events that night at Ford's Theatre. The woodcut shown at right, of John Wilkes Booth aiming his pistol at an unsuspecting Lincoln, and those on the following pages limning the escape, were published in *Frank Leslie's Illustrated Newspaper* beginning in late April of 1865.

After shooting the President and overcoming Major Rathbone's efforts to detain him, Booth vaults from the railing of the theater box to the stage below. As Booth leaped, one of his spurs caught in the U.S. Treasury Guards flag that was suspended from the center column of the box, ripping the flag slightly *(below)*. Booth landed off-balance, breaking a bone in his left leg.

Exaggerated accounts of Booth's retreat across the stage circulated after the assassination. Booth had hobbled out on a broken leg; one story, however, had him sauntering to the footlights to proclaim *"Sic semper tyrannis!" (right)*, then striding defiantly away. Another version told of an accomplice tossing Booth a rope and then pulling him out of sight.

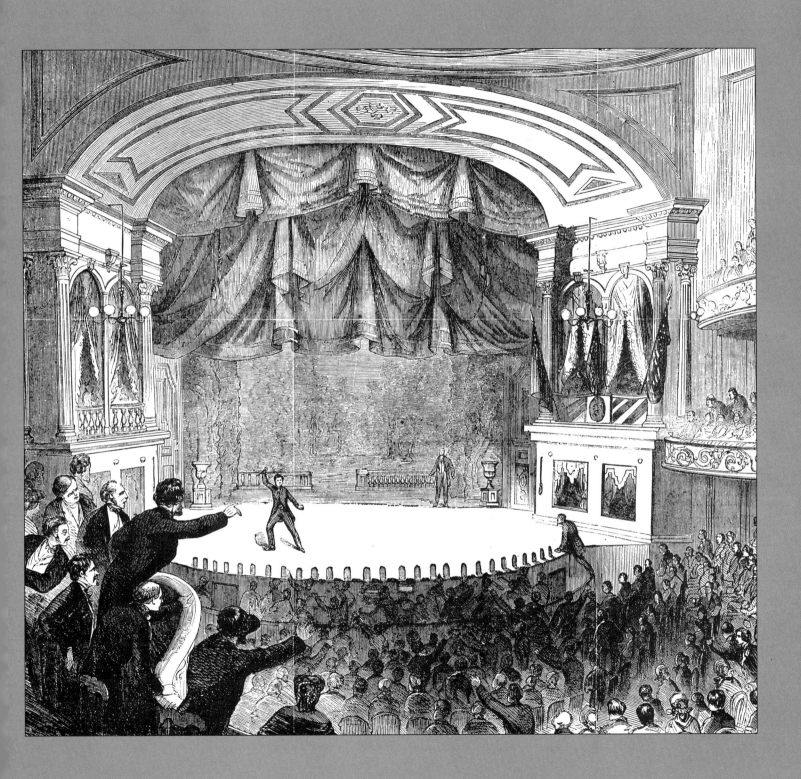

In this contemporary woodcut, Booth is shown fleeing on horseback, with a member of the audience in close pursuit. The actual getaway was not that close: Booth

had galloped off on a waiting horse before his pursuers reached the alley.

Additional help arrived in the person of Dr. Charles Sabin Taft, also 23, who had clambered onto the stage from his orchestra seat and then had been lifted by others to a point where he could reach the railing of the presidential box. Together the two doctors began applying artificial respiration. After compressing Lincoln's tongue to clear the windpipe, Leale started thrusting against his diaphragm while Taft lifted and lowered the patient's arms. Nothing. Working desperately against time, Leale massaged Lincoln's chest. Again, nothing. Bending over, Leale put his mouth to the President's, blowing again and again as hard as he could, mouth to mouth and then mouth to nostrils.

At last Abraham Lincoln's breathing resumed feebly on its own. The young doctor rose to an erect kneeling position and watched his patient intently. Finally he got slowly to his feet, satisfied "that the President could continue independent breathing and that instant death would not occur." But he knew better than to hold out any hope. "His wound is mortal," he said. "It is impossible for him to recover."

Two other physicians, Albert F. A. King and Charles A. Gatch, arrived in the now-crowded box. "We must get him to the nearest bed," Leale told them. Someone suggested the White House, six blocks away. No, said Leale, the President "would die on the way." So, without knowing where they were going, the doctors and some soldiers lifted Abraham Lincoln and, with Leale going first and supporting the head, moved out of the presidential box. Around the dress circle, down the stairs and into the street they went — out of what Mary Lincoln in her grief would call "that terrible, terrible theater."

A Night of Tears and Violence

Opposite Ford's Theatre, in a four-story house at 453 10th Street, a tailor named William Petersen kept a shop in the basement and rented rooms to five male lodgers on the floors above. In one of the rooms, on the second floor, a youthful War Department employee was resting on his bed when the men bearing President Lincoln came out of the theater lobby and into the street.

Although Henry Safford had not yet heard about the assassination, the cries in the street told him that something had happened. He jumped up and rushed to the window. When Safford understood that the President had been shot, he ran downstairs, lit a candle and, stepping out onto the front stoop, called: "Bring him in here!"

The people thronging 10th Street were in a frenzy. When one man rashly shouted that he was glad Lincoln had been gunned down, he was beaten and nearly lynched before the police saved him. Through the tide of humanity the procession of doctors and soldiers moved slowly, trying their best to protect the wounded President from the jostling of the crowd. A light rain had begun to fall. At intervals they stopped while Dr. Charles Leale removed newly formed blood clots from Lincoln's wound. It took the little group about five minutes to cross the street and mount the steps to the Petersen house.

Dr. Leale asked Henry Safford to lead them to the best room available. One of the soldiers carrying the President, artilleryman Jacob J. Soles of Pennsylvania, remembered that they went down a long hallway and into a room near the middle of the building.

"There was a bed in that room," said Soles, "and we laid him on the bed." The time was about 10:45 p.m., roughly half an hour after Booth had fired his single shot.

The room was about 10 by 18 feet — narrow, low-ceilinged and dark. Normally it was occupied by William T. Clark, a Massachusetts soldier on duty in Washington with the Quartermaster Department. Clark was out celebrating the Union victory this particular evening, and the room was empty. One of its former inhabitants, ironically, had been an actor friend of John Wilkes Booth. In fact, the bed on which the soldiers placed Lincoln had once been used by Booth himself for an afternoon nap. With its cornhusk mattress cradled in ropes, clean sheets and red-white-and-blue worsted coverlet adorned in each corner by eagles, the bed presented only one problem: It was too short for Lincoln's six feet four inches.

So that the President's full length might be accommodated, Dr. Leale ordered that the footboard of the walnut spool bed be removed. The other doctors tried their best, but the bed was sturdily built and the footboard refused to budge. It was therefore necessary to arrange the President in a diagonal position. When Secretaries Edwin Stanton and Gideon Welles pushed through the crowd in the corridor and entered the room, they found the patient resting with his head in one corner of the bed and his feet near the opposite corner, protruding over the side. For the two Cabinet members, the sight was one more shock in what had already been a nightmarish evening: They had just come

SURRAT.   BOOTH.   HAROLD.

War Department, Washington, April 20, 1865,

 # $100,000 REWARD!

THE MURDERER

Of our late beloved President, Abraham Lincoln,

IS STILL AT LARGE.

$50,000 REWARD

Will be paid by this Department for his apprehension, in addition to any reward offered by Municipal Authorities or State Executives.

$25,000 REWARD

Will be paid for the apprehension of JOHN H. SURRATT, one of Booth's Accomplices.

$25,000 REWARD

Will be paid for the apprehension of David C. Harold, another of Booth's accomplices.

LIBERAL REWARDS will be paid for any information that shall conduce to the arrest of either of the above-named criminals, or their accomplices.

All persons harboring or secreting the said persons, or either of them, or aiding or assisting their concealment or escape, will be treated as accomplices in the murder of the President and the attempted assassination of the Secretary of State, and shall be subject to trial before a Military Commission and the punishment of DEATH.

Let the stain of innocent blood be removed from the land by the arrest and punishment of the murderers.

All good citizens are exhorted to aid public justice on this occasion. Every man should consider his own conscience charged with this solemn duty, and rest neither night nor day until it be accomplished.

EDWIN M. STANTON, Secretary of War.

DESCRIPTIONS.—BOOTH is Five Feet 7 or 8 inches high, slender build, high forehead, black hair, black eyes, and wears a heavy black moustache.

JOHN H. SURRAT is about 5 feet, 9 inches. Hair rather thin and dark; eyes rather light; no beard. Would weigh 145 or 150 pounds. Complexion rather pale and clear, with color in his cheeks. Wore light clothes of fine quality. Shoulders square; cheek bones rather prominent; chin narrow; ears projecting at the top; forehead rather low and square, but broad. Parts his hair on the right side; neck rather long. His lips are firmly set. A slim man.

DAVID C. HAROLD is five feet six inches high, hair dark, eyes dark, eyebrows rather heavy, full face, nose short, hand short and fleshy, feet small, instep high, round bodied, naturally quick and active, slightly closes his eyes when looking at a person.

NOTICE.—In addition to the above, State and other authorities have offered rewards amounting to almost one hundred thousand dollars, making an aggregate of about TWO HUNDRED THOUSAND DOLLARS.

A War Department poster offers large rewards for the capture of Booth, Surratt and Herold.

Men carrying the President step cautiously into the street in front of Ford's Theatre. The artist who painted this scene was on his balcony across from Ford's that night, sketching one of Washington's many victory parades *(right)*, when the cry went up, "The President has been shot!"

1848

from William Seward's home, where the Secretary of State had also been assailed and now lay grievously wounded.

The assault on Seward had occurred at almost the same moment as Booth's attack on the President. As investigators reconstructed the sequence, Lewis Paine arrived outside the Sewards' three-story mansion on Lafayette Square, across from the White House, at 10:10 p.m. He was slouched on top of Booth's one-eyed horse and accompanied by David Herold, who was serving as his guide. Herold, who would not participate in the attack, would soon join Booth on his flight southward.

Paine tied his horse to a tree, mounted the low doorstep of the Seward residence and rang the bell. Inside the house, in his third-floor sickroom, the Secretary of State was drifting in a hazy zone between drug-induced sleep and the wakefulness caused by his pain. Attending him were his daughter Fanny and Private George F. Robinson, a soldier from Maine who had been assigned to nursing duty while recovering from his own wounds. In a nearby room, Seward's son Frederick and his daughter-in-law were spending a quiet evening; another son, Major Augustus Seward, was napping in his bedroom so that he would be rested when, at 11 o'clock, it came time for him to relieve Fanny at their father's bedside.

William Bell, a black servant, answered the door. He beheld a large man with massive shoulders and a "very red" face that was partly concealed by a brown hat pulled down over one eye. Keeping one hand in the pocket of his light overcoat, Paine used the other to display a small package that, he said, contained medicine from Dr. Tullio Verdi. The

physician, he declared, had ordered him to give it to Seward personally, along with dosage instructions.

Bell protested. Seward, he said, was far too ill to be bothered by a deliveryman. Paine shouldered his way into the house. "He looked pretty fiery out of his eyes at me," Bell recalled. Cowed, the houseman started up the stairs. Paine followed, his heavy boots clomping loudly. At her father's bedside, Fanny Seward heard the noise and indignantly said to the male nurse, " Wouldn't you think that person would be more quiet coming up to a sickroom?"

Also disturbed, Frederick Seward came out of his room and from the top of the stairs confronted Paine, who explained his errand. It would be impossible to see the sick man, said young Seward — his father was just going to sleep. But at Paine's insistence Frederick looked in to make sure his father was really sleeping, thus disclosing the location of the sickroom. When Seward came back, repeating that his father could not be disturbed, Paine suddenly became conciliatory. "Very well, sir," he said meekly, "I will go." He turned and started down the stairs. Then, cursing, he whirled, a large Navy revolver in his hand. At pointblank range Paine pulled the trigger. The weapon failed to fire.

With a roar of rage, Paine hurled himself at Frederick Seward, savagely pounding him with the revolver. Seward fell against the banister, his skull fractured in two places. Paine hammered him to the floor, breaking the pistol in the process. Yet Frederick continued to grapple with his assailant, collapsing only as the two of them reached the doorway of William Seward's room. The servant, William Bell, had rushed down the stairs and

95

outside the house, shouting "Murder! Murder!" Finding no immediate help, he started running toward the nearby offices of Major General Christopher C. Augur, commander of the military Department of Washington, to raise the alarm.

Hearing the disturbance on the stairs, Private Robinson opened the door of the sickroom to see what was going on. Paine, who had flung aside his pistol, rushed at him with a bowie knife. Robinson went down, blood streaming from his forehead. Paine shoved Fanny Seward out of the way and leaped onto Secretary Seward's bed. He flailed frenziedly with his knife, ripping at the Secretary's face. One stab laid open Seward's entire right cheek, exposing his tongue. Another gashed the left side of his neck.

By now Robinson had staggered to his feet and caught Paine from behind. Up and down went Paine's knife hand. And again. Blood poured from Robinson's shoulder, which had been cut twice to the bone; nonetheless he clutched at Paine. Major Augustus Seward came hurrying from his room, clad only in his shirt and underdrawers. Seeing one man holding another at the foot of the bed, he at first concluded in his sleep-dazed state that George Robinson was trying to restrain the delirious Secretary Seward. Augustus seized the clothing of the person being held but knew immediately "from his size and strength" that it was not his father. While Paine struck savagely at his head with the knife, Major Seward tried desperately to push the assailant out of the room. During the brief, furious struggle, the major would recall, Paine kept repeating "in an intense but not strong voice, the words 'I'm mad! I'm mad!' " When the swaying group reached the hallway, Paine broke free and

Frederick Seward, on the landing, bars Lewis Paine from his father's sickroom while Paine, having turned as if to leave the house, draws his revolver to attack young Seward. Frederick lay in a coma for two and a half days following Paine's vicious beating; he recovered, however, and lived for another 50 years.

plunged down the stairs. At the bottom, he was confronted by William Seward's State Department messenger, who had been roused by the noise. Scarcely pausing, Paine stabbed the messenger in the back and ran out of the house.

By the time Paine reached the street, David Herold had already departed. Paine swung into the saddle of his horse; the knife he threw in the gutter. All told, he had been in the house little more than five minutes. As he rode away on Vermont Avenue, seemingly in no great hurry, he crossed the path of William Bell, who was returning to the house with a couple of soldiers. Bell followed the would-be assassin on foot for a few blocks. Finally Paine spurred his horse and galloped into the night.

Back at the Seward home, the Secretary of State lay unconscious, apparently beyond

Shaking off Seward's army nurse (*left*) and two of Seward's sons, would-be assassin Lewis Paine slashes at the bedridden Secretary of State. Armed with a revolver and a bowie knife (*shown at three fifths its actual size, at left*), the powerful Paine wounded every man he met in the house, except the servant William Bell; all of them survived.

help. His son Augustus, assisted by the severely wounded male nurse, removed Seward's clothing and felt for a pulse. Just then William Seward opened his eyes and spoke firmly. "I am not dead," he said. "Send for a surgeon, send for the police, close the house." Seward, like Paine's other victims, would miraculously survive.

Vice President Johnson, the other public figure slated for assassination that bloody evening, would survive as well — thanks to the qualms of George Atzerodt. Although he was a man of few scruples, Atzerodt was not a killer. As the evening drew on, he became less and less happy about his assigned role in the assassination plot. Feeling entrapped in Booth's scheme, he did what came most naturally: He got drunk to forget his troubles.

When the time for the murder came, Atzerodt was in the bar of Kirkwood House,

drinking whiskey. The reluctant assassin had a large bowie knife stuck in his belt, and Andrew Johnson was preparing for bed in the same building. But poor Atzerodt, with his "pigeon liver" — the phrase came from his defense lawyer — let 10:15 come and go and went on drinking. He was "guzzling like a Falstaff," according to the lawyer.

It was probably not until after 11 o'clock in the evening that Atzerodt, out on the street between stops at various saloons, saw a cavalry troop gallop frantically by. Obviously, some sort of emergency had arisen — and even in his inebriated condition, Atzerodt well knew what it might be. In his confusion and fright, he flung away his knife, which came to rest in the street beneath a carriage step, and looked for a way to get out of the center of town quickly.

Having foolishly returned his rented horse to its stable, Atzerodt was without transportation. On Pennsylvania Avenue he boarded a horse-drawn streetcar bound for the Navy Yard. A fellow passenger turned out to be an acquaintance, Washington Briscoe, who managed a store at the yard. Atzerodt pleaded for permission to sleep overnight in the store. Briscoe, however, thought he was behaving "like a loafer" and refused. Afraid to go back to his room at Kirkwood House, Atzerodt wearily turned around and made his way to his old lodging, sleazy Pennsylvania House. He arrived there at 2 a.m., registered and went to bed in a room with five other men. At about the same hour his intended victim, Vice President Johnson, was arriving at the Petersen house to visit the stricken President.

Throughout that terrible night, as many as 90 people, including 16 physicians, would crowd into the tiny room where Lincoln lay dying. One of the first was Mary Lincoln, who arrived immediately after the doctors. "Where is my dear husband?" she cried. "Where is he?" When she saw him inert and apparently lifeless, her cries grew louder, and the doctors, desiring to get about their business in an atmosphere of relative calm, requested that she be taken away.

Only now, in the room with the perfume of lilacs wafting in through the window, could the doctors remove Lincoln's remaining clothes and perform a methodical examination. They found that the President's fluttering heart was beating at 44 weak strokes per minute. The pupil of one eye was greatly dilated, the pupil of the other was contracted, and neither eye was in the slightest responsive to light.

Accounts differ as to where the bullet had come to rest. "The course of the ball," read one subsequent medical report, "was obliquely forward toward the right eye, crossing the brain in an oblique manner and lodging a few inches behind that eye. In the track of the wound were found fragments of bone driven forward by the ball, which was embedded in the anterior lobe of the left hemisphere of the brain." It was clearly a fatal wound and yet Lincoln lingered, to the amazement of the doctors. "The wonderful vitality exhibited by the late President was one of the most interesting and remarkable circumstances connected with the case," wrote Dr. Charles Taft. "It was the opinion of the surgeons in charge that most patients would have died in two hours."

Vitality aside, the doctors were struck by Abraham Lincoln's marvelous physique. In his clothes, he had seemed a gaunt, loose-jointed sort of man; naked, he looked powerful, with smooth, strong muscles and not an ounce of superfluous fat. Indeed, as Dr. Leale commented, the President might have served as a model for Michelangelo's *Moses*. Gideon Welles was reminded of a "giant sufferer" whose large arms "were of a size which one would scarce have expected from his spare appearance."

But the President's body was growing cold, especially at his lower extremities. To provide warmth, the physicians packed bottles filled with hot water around Lincoln's legs. Mustard plasters were placed on his upper body, and army blankets were heated and used to cover him. At Mrs. Lincoln's request the family physician, Dr. Robert King Stone, a dignified gentleman in a top hat, had been summoned. He too examined the President's wound, probing it with the little finger of his right hand. Then he pronounced the case hopeless. "He is tenacious and he will resist," Stone declared. "But death will close the scene."

At first Gideon Welles found that grim prognosis hard to believe. For almost the whole night, Welles remained in the room, seated in a chair at the foot of Lincoln's bed and gazing quietly at the President's recumbent form. During the first hour, as Welles subsequently wrote in his diary, "his

Fanny Seward (*left*), the only daughter of Secretary of State William Henry Seward (*right*), was at her father's bedside when Lewis Paine entered the house on his murderous mission. Secretary Seward survived the attack but his wife, her frail health broken by the shock, died two months later; Fanny, who had never been robust, succumbed the following year.

features were calm and striking. I had never seen them appear to better advantage." Then a terrible transformation took place. Lincoln's right eyeball began to bulge from its socket. As the flesh around the eye turned purple, Dr. Leale noted other discouraging symptoms: "Left side of patient's face begins to twitch. The mouth is pulled sharply to left in a jeer. After 15 minutes it stops."

Unable to do anything else, Leale held the President's hand in his own. The doctor wrote later that he wanted to let Abraham Lincoln "in his blindness know, if possible, that he was in touch with humanity and had a friend."

All the while, the stream of visitors continued to push in and out of the room. Among them was Massachusetts Senator Charles Sumner, who had now forgotten his heated, abolitionist criticisms of Lincoln's more moderate policies. Although Sumner was not given to displays of human compassion, he had gone to the White House, picked up Robert Todd Lincoln and escorted the young man to his father's bedside.

Seated near the head of the President's bed, the Senator spoke gently to Lincoln, only to be interrupted by one of the doctors. "It's no use," the physician said. "He can't hear you. He is dead." Looking closely at the President, Sumner protested, "No, he isn't dead. Look at his face, he's breathing." The physician shook his head and said, "It will never be anything more than this." Hearing that, Robert Lincoln burst into tears, and Charles Sumner took him in his arms. A little while later, after Robert had gone to the front parlor to be with his mother, the austere Sumner gave way to his own grief. One who was present remembered him "sobbing like a woman, with his head bowed down almost on the pillow of the bed on which the President was lying."

Mary Lincoln was, understandably, in a piteous condition. She spent much of the long night prostrate on a sofa in the small parlor that had become her waiting room. Once she mused aloud to herself: "Why did he not shoot me instead of my husband? I have tried to be so careful of him." Then, in a determined voice, Mary Lincoln declared, "I must go with him!" And finally: "How can it be so?"

At intervals Mrs. Lincoln walked, with assistance, down the hallway to her husband's bedside. The doctors, who were warned of her coming to the room, hastily covered the pillows with clean towels to conceal the fact that they were soaked with her husband's blood. Once she looked at the body and fainted. Another time she loudly implored the unconscious President "Live! You must live!" Finally, about 3 a.m., she again entered the room and, flinging her body on Lincoln's, begged, "Love, live but one moment to speak to our children—oh! oh! that my little Taddy might see his father before he dies." From Lincoln came a deep, rattling gasp for breath, so alarming Mary that she fell to the floor with a scream. At that, Secretary Stanton ordered that she be taken away and not readmitted to the President's sickroom. It was the last time Mary Todd Lincoln would see her husband alive.

The President began to fail noticeably as rain continued to splatter on the windows of the Petersen house, and dawn approached. At 6:40 a.m., Dr. Albert King jotted in a notebook that Lincoln's breaths were "prolonged and groaning—a deep, softly sonorous cooing sound at the end of each expiration." Five minutes later, King wrote:

"Respiration uneasy and grunting, lower jaw relaxed." At 7 o'clock, Lincoln was "still breathing at long pauses." Minutes passed. Then, about nine hours after Booth's bullet had entered his brain, the President's chest rose, fell and did not rise again. At 7:22 a.m. on the morning of April 15, 1865, Abraham Lincoln was dead.

The Reverend Phineas Densmore Gurley, pastor of the Presbyterian church attended by the Lincoln family, led the group assembled at the Petersen house in prayer. With the exception of Mary Lincoln, none of the mourners was more visibly moved than Stanton. He stood with his chin in his left

Assistant Surgeon Charles A. Leale, the first doctor to examine Lincoln, had graduated from medical school just six weeks earlier. He had come to Ford's that night expressly to see Lincoln and "study the characteristics of the saviour of his country."

In an 1860s equivalent of a banner headline, the New York *Herald* for April 15 trumpets the news of Lincoln's assassination and the attack on Seward. The front page also carries a report on the recent Union victory at Petersburg and a proclamation from the fugitive Jefferson Davis, who vows never to make peace with "the infamous invader."

THE NEW YORK HERALD.

WHOLE NO. 10,456.   NEW YORK, SATURDAY, APRIL 15, 1865.   PRICE FOUR CENTS.

IMPORTANT.

ASSASSINATION

OF

PRESIDENT LINCOLN.

The President Shot at the Theatre Last Evening.

SECRETARY SEWARD

DAGGERED IN HIS BED,

BUT

NOT MORTALLY WOUNDED.

Clarence and Frederick Seward Badly Hurt.

ESCAPE OF THE ASSASSINS.

Intense Excitement in Washington.

Scene at the Deathbed of Mr. Lincoln.

J. Wilkes Booth, the Actor, the Alleged Assassin of the President.

THE OFFICIAL DESPATCH.

THE HERALD DESPATCHES.

THE PRESS DESPATCHES.

Additional Details of the Assassination.

THE STATE CAPITAL.

IMPORTANT FROM SOUTH AMERICA.

News from San Francisco.

THE REBELS.

JEFF. DAVIS AT DANVILLE.

His Latest Appeal to His Deluded Followers.

He Thinks the Fall of Richmond a Blessing in Disguise, as it Leaves the Rebel Armies Free to Move from Point to Point.

He Vainly Promises to Hold Virginia at All Hazards.

Lee and His Army Supposed to be Safe.

Breckinridge and the Rest of Davis' Cabinet Reach Danville Safely.

The Organ of Governor Vance, of North Carolina, Advises the Submission of the Rebels to President Lincoln's Terms, &c., &c., &c.

Jeff. Davis' Last Proclamation.

The Organ of Governor Vance, of North Carolina, Advising General Lee to Submit on Mr. Lincoln's Terms.

hand, crying quietly and steadily. He also pulled himself together faster than the others—for he had taken charge of the United States government.

Stanton had spent precious little time that night by the bedside of the President. Hardly had he gotten to the Petersen house than he had set up headquarters in a bedroom near the room where Lincoln lay. From that post, according to a War Department subordinate, Stanton had "instantly assumed charge of everything near and remote, civil and military, and began issuing orders in that autocratic manner so supremely necessary to the occasion. He continued throughout the night, acting as president, secretary of war, secretary of state, commander in chief, comforter and dictator."

Already in force were orders from Stanton halting all southbound passenger trains from Washington; forbidding all boats on the Potomac River from touching shore south of Alexandria; posting guards outside the homes of Cabinet officers; mobilizing the

In an engraving (*opposite*) of the room where Lincoln spent his last hours, members of the government maintain a deathbed vigil. Seated at far left are Secretary of the Navy Welles and Secretary of War Stanton; Surgeon General Joseph K. Barnes cradles the dying President's head, while Lincoln's son Robert wipes tears from his own eyes. The photograph below, which was made later that morning, shows the bed empty, its pillow soaked with Lincoln's blood.

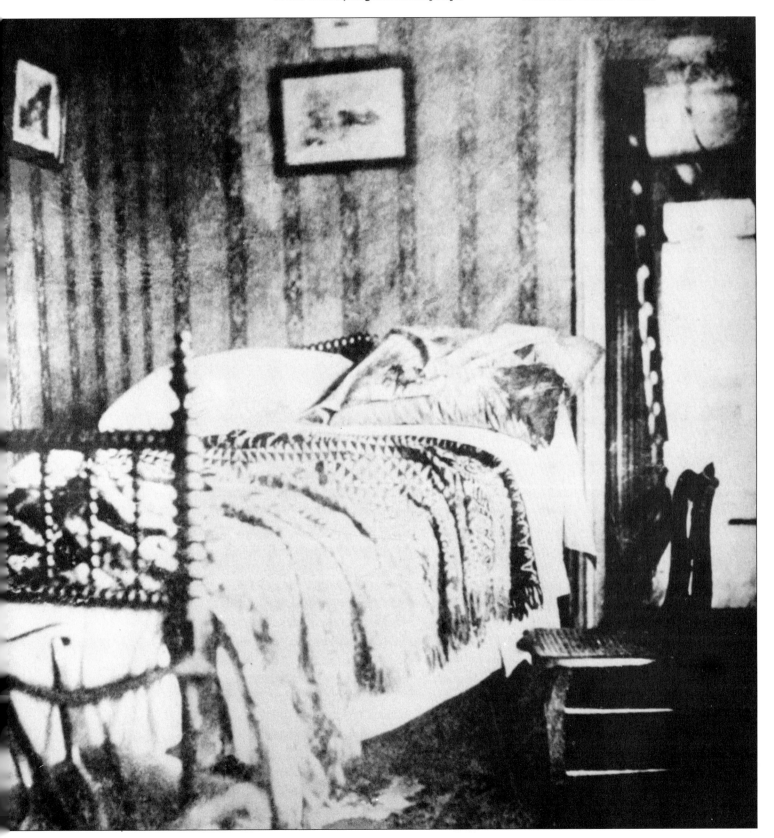

Washington fire brigade against mass arson; putting 8,000 Washington troops on alert; and closing down Ford's Theatre. In Stanton's hands were pages of shorthand testimony taken during the night from witnesses who had been in the cast and audience at Ford's Theatre. Many of them reported that they had clearly recognized the matinee idol Booth as he had leaped from the presidential box. Their collective testimony was sufficient, observed the clerk who transcribed it, "to hang Wilkes Booth, the assassin, higher than ever Haman hung."

At 3 o'clock in the morning, the first cable had gone out naming John Wilkes Booth as the killer. Now that Abraham Lincoln was dead, and while preparations were being made to remove his body to the White House and swear in Andrew Johnson as President, Stanton turned his full attention to the pursuit of the conspirators.

In fact, Federal authorities had already had John Wilkes Booth within their grasp and had let him slip by. That frustrating but understandable blunder had occurred only minutes after the assassin fled Ford's Theatre. His route took him from F Street across Judiciary Square to Pennsylvania Avenue. Booth was seen riding fast just south of the Capitol grounds and on toward the Navy Yard Bridge, at the foot of 11th Street in southeast Washington.

In his guardhouse at the Washington end of the bridge, Sergeant Silas T. Cobb was unaware of the fear and confusion that had swept the national capital within minutes of the shot fired at Ford's Theatre. As a wartime security measure, the Navy Yard Bridge had been shut off to traffic after 9 o'clock in the evening. Now, though, with the conflict all but over, enforcement of the regulation had been relaxed.

About 10:45 p.m. on the tense night of April 14, Sergeant Cobb and his two sentries heard the hoofbeats of a horse, ridden hard, drumming down 11th Street toward the bridge. As the animal was pulled to a halt at the sentry gate, one of the soldiers stepped out of the guardhouse, grasped the reins, and led the horse and its rider into the light. At that moment, John Wilkes Booth did something extremely peculiar for a man who was on the run.

"My name is Booth," he said promptly when asked his identity. He even volunteered the direction in which he was going — toward southern Maryland — thus providing information that would be invaluable to his pursuers. John Wilkes Booth's story was that he had been in Washington on an errand and had started late toward his home near Beantown so that he could ride by the light of the moon. Cobb thought he was "a proper person to pass," and he waved the assassin on into the Maryland night.

Within about 10 minutes another man on horseback appeared at the gate, said that his name was Smith and gave his address as White Plains, Maryland. Asked what had brought him out at this late hour of the night, the man "made use of a rather indelicate expression," remembered Sergeant Cobb, "and said that he had been in bad company." Again the sentry gate swung open, and David Herold rode through.

Some distance beyond the Navy Yard Bridge, Herold caught up with Booth. They exchanged horses: By then, the assassin's lower leg was paining him terribly, and Herold's mount had an easier gait. Together the two rode southeast toward the tavern in Sur-

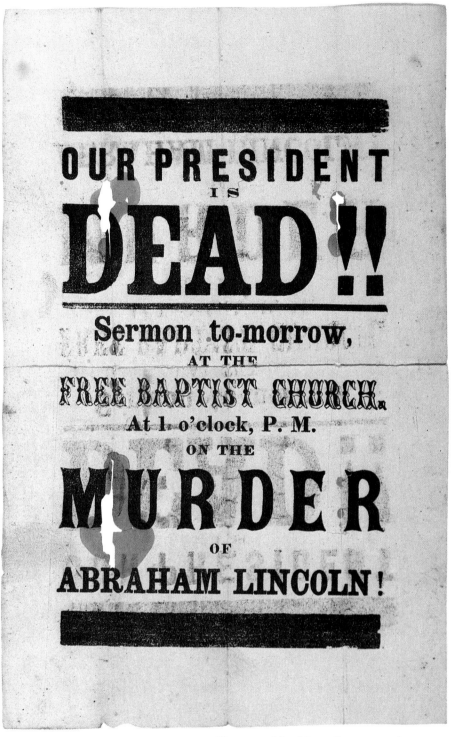

OUR PRESIDENT
IS
DEAD!!
Sermon to-morrow,
AT THE
FREE BAPTIST CHURCH,
At 1 o'clock, P. M.
ON THE
MURDER
OF
ABRAHAM LINCOLN!

A church broadside announces a sermon on the death of Lincoln — the subject of every minister's text on Easter Day, 1865. Many clergymen called the assassination "the will of God," and some compared the martyred president to Jesus Christ; more than a few called for vengeance against the South.

they were leaving, Booth told Lloyd, "I am pretty sure we have assassinated the President and Secretary Seward."

Moving southeast still, the fugitives came to a small crossroads village, known only by the initials T.B., between 1 and 2 a.m. Herold was familiar with the place, but they kept going toward Bryantown. Booth's broken leg clearly needed medical attention, and it was natural that he would seek out Dr. Samuel Mudd, in whose home near Bryantown he had once spent a night.

About 4 a.m., Dr. Mudd was wakened by the sound of pounding on the door of his house. According to his own subsequent testimony, the doctor went to the door in his nightshirt and, without opening it, asked who was there. David Herold called out that they were two strangers riding to Washington and that one of them had hurt his ankle in a bad fall from his horse. Cautiously Dr. Mudd let them enter.

The doctor would claim that Herold had introduced himself by the name of Henson and his companion as Tyser or Tyson. At no time, Dr. Mudd would insist, had he recognized his patient as John Wilkes Booth. But Mudd changed his story just before his death many years later; he asserted to an associate that he had recognized Booth on sight but did not realize that he was a fugitive.

With Herold lending a hand, Dr. Mudd assisted the injured man to a sofa in the parlor and then to a bed upstairs. With a sharp surgical instrument he slit Booth's left boot. Easing off boot and sock, Mudd examined the badly swollen leg. He diagnosed a fracture of the fibula and fashioned a makeshift wooden splint. By 4:45 a.m., the job was done. Leaving Booth in a half-stupor, Dr. Mudd returned to his interrupted slumber.

rattsville owned by Mary Surratt and operated by John Lloyd.

When they arrived shortly after midnight, they found Lloyd asleep and befuddled by drink. He had been "right smart in liquor that afternoon," Lloyd said, "and after night" he got more so. Picking up one of the carbines hidden there earlier by John Surratt, and a pair of field glasses, the fugitives gulped down some whiskey and rode on. As

Mudd did not sleep for very long. Rising early, he took breakfast with Herold. Booth declined to eat the food that was brought up to him. After their meal together, Herold asked Mudd to give him directions for the shortest route to the Potomac River. The doctor led Herold outside and pointed to a cart path leading through Zekiah Swamp, a forbidding wilderness of bogs and thickets, which stretched southwest from Mudd's house toward the Potomac. A Union officer who searched the area would write that "even a hunted murderer would shrink from hiding there; serpents and slimy lizards are the only living denizens."

In the afternoon, at Herold's request, Mudd had his hired farmhand make a set of crutches for Booth; then Mudd and Herold set off for Bryantown to look for a carriage, in which Booth could ride less painfully than in a saddle. On the way, however, Herold suddenly declared that he and Booth would continue their journey on horseback; he returned to Mudd's farmhouse while the doctor went on to Bryantown to mail some letters and to purchase several items from the local store.

Back at Mudd's house, Herold informed the doctor's wife that he and his companion were leaving. As John Wilkes Booth struggled slowly down the stairs, Mrs. Mudd noted that his face "presented a picture of agony." About this time, Dr. Mudd returned from Bryantown, having just learned—he claimed much later—that President Lincoln had been assassinated and that Booth was a wanted man. He said that at that point he ordered both Booth and Herold off his place.

About 5 p.m., the two fugitives rode into the gloom of Zekiah Swamp. They soon got lost, wandering around until about 9 p.m.,

when they turned up at the cabin of a black tobacco farmer, Oswell Swann. Herold offered Swann $12 to guide them across the swamp to the home of Samuel Cox, a wealthy farmer and a known Confederate sympathizer. It was after midnight when Swann brought the weary riders to Cox's front door.

With Cox, Booth felt comfortable enough to identify himself as the assassin of President Lincoln. Yet, zealot though he may have been, Cox was too prudent to allow Booth and Herold to remain in his home. Instead he gave them a meal, sent them to a dense pine thicket about two miles away and dispatched his adopted son to fetch a Confederate agent named Thomas A. Jones. A daring and resourceful man, Jones had helped many Confederate couriers cross the Potomac during the War, and he knew the shoreline well.

Approaching the thicket, Jones gave a whistle. In response Herold emerged from the tangled brush, pointing a carbine. When Jones explained that he came from Cox, Herold led him through the undergrowth to a clearing. There Booth lay on the cold, wet ground, his weapons beside him. Jones's immediate impression, as he told it, was that he had never seen "a more strikingly handsome man," even though Booth's face "bore the evident traces of suffering." Jones was touched by Booth's plight, "murderer though I knew him to be." He decided to do all that he could to accomplish "what then seemed to be the well-nigh hopeless task of getting him to Virginia." Holding out his hand in gratitude, the assassin dramatically declared to Jones, "John Wilkes Booth will never be taken alive."

Knowing that the area was already swarming with soldiers, Jones told the fugitives

Lieutenant Henry M. Brewster (*inset*) was the officer in charge of the Veteran Reserve Corps guard that patrolled the Navy Yard Bridge the night Booth and Herold fled across it into Maryland. The photograph below, attributed to Mathew Brady, shows the wooden span from the Maryland side of the river.

that they would have to remain in the thicket until it was safe to cross the Potomac River. He also advised Booth and Herold to kill their horses: This would prevent the animals' neighing from betraying them.

For five days and four frigid, miserable nights, John Wilkes Booth and David Herold lay hidden in the bush — and during that period, the Federal authorities rounded up most of their accomplices.

In the chaotic hours immediately following President Lincoln's murder, the burden of pursuing his assassin fell on General Augur, the local military commander, and on Major A. C. Richards, head of the Washington police force. Long before the drizzly dawn, they had between them acquired the names of George Atzerodt, David Herold, John Surratt and, possibly, Ned Spangler. The two officers owed this investigative success partially to good police work, and in equal measure to sheer luck.

The first break came shortly after midnight with the visit of a detective named John Lee to Kirkwood House, where Vice President Johnson was staying. Sent to help protect Johnson, Lee examined the hotel premises and then dropped by the bar for a drink. There he ran into an acquaintance who told him that a "suspicious-looking" man had signed in the previous day. When he checked the hotel register, Lee saw the name G. A. Atzerodt. He decided it might be a good idea to inspect Atzerodt's room.

Since Atzerodt had taken the only key, Lee broke through the door, began to search and almost immediately found several items of interest: a loaded pistol under a pillow, a bowie knife between the bedclothes and the mattress, three boxes of cartridges in a draw-

er and a Montreal bankbook made out in the name of J. Wilkes Booth.

Even as Detective John Lee was examining these items, official interest in George Atzerodt was further whetted by the arrival at General Augur's headquarters of John Fletcher, a stable foreman. For the past few days, Atzerodt and David Herold had been Fletcher's steady customers. Now Fletcher was angry and was bitterly complaining that the horse Herold had promised to have back to him by 8 o'clock on the previous evening had not been returned. Indeed, Fletcher had seen David Herold riding the horse past Willard's Hotel at 10:25 p.m. and had pursued him as far as the Navy Yard Bridge. In his complaint, Fletcher gave the investigators not only Herold's name but also that of his sidekick, George Atzerodt.

Fletcher's tale inspired Augur to question all the liverymen in the area. James Pumphrey told about renting Booth the skittish little mare he rode on the night of the assassination; liveryman Brooke Stabler provided the name of John Surratt as someone for whom he kept horses and with whom Booth and Atzerodt were intimate. Obviously the same names were recurring with unusual frequency. Other tips accumulating at police headquarters also identified Surratt as an associate of Booth's. During the early morning hours of April 15, Detective John A. W. Clarvoe led a squad of four men to Mary Surratt's boardinghouse at 541 H Street, with orders to arrest John Surratt and, if he was there, John Wilkes Booth.

Clarvoe yanked on the bellpull of the darkened house about 2:15 a.m. Louis Weichmann came to the door, his feet bare and his nightshirt tucked into the trousers he had hastily pulled on. While the detectives start-

The riding boot that Dr. Samuel Mudd (*below*) had cut from Booth's swollen leg was left behind when Booth and Herold departed. Mudd did not mention the boot to the detectives who questioned him until they called a second time and began to search his house; then the boot, which had Booth's name written inside, led to the doctor's arrest.

ed searching the house, Weichmann went to call Mrs. Surratt, then returned to demand the meaning of the intrusion. When told, mistakenly, that Booth had killed the President and Surratt the Secretary of State, Weichmann melodramatically threw up his hands, lurched about the room and cried, "My God! I see it all."

He repeated the news to Mary Surratt as soon as the landlady emerged from her room. "My God, Mr. Weichmann," she said, "do not tell me so!" To Clarvoe, watching closely, the woman's startled reaction seemed genuine. She admitted she had seen Booth as recently as the day before, but she insisted that her son had been gone about two weeks and that she did not know where he was. Clarvoe and his men departed.

Weichmann returned to his bed, where he spent a sleepless night. Immediately after breakfast he went to police headquarters and revealed all he knew about the Surratt house and its occupants. Held in a sort of protective custody, Weichmann slept that night on the floor of the police station. On Monday, April 17, he was sent with police officers to Montreal to assist in the hunt for his old roommate, John Surratt.

Surratt, at the time of Lincoln's assassination, had been in Elmira, New York, at the behest of Confederate officials in Canada; he was to scout a local prisoner-of-war camp and assess the chances of a successful breakout by the Confederates held captive there. On hearing that the Federal authorities had posted a $25,000 reward for his arrest, Surratt hurried back across the Canadian border. On a Montreal street he actually got a glimpse of his "Nemesis," Louis Weichmann. Surratt promptly went underground, not to surface again for nearly two years. His absence would play a critical role in deciding the fate of his mother.

On the same day that Louis Weichmann left for Montreal, the arrests began in earnest. Ned Spangler, the tosspot stagehand, was quickly picked up by the authorities because of his known friendship with John Wilkes Booth and his hostility to Abraham Lincoln. Samuel Arnold was taken into custody because a letter signed by him had been found in Booth's trunk at the National Hotel. In Baltimore, police arrested garrulous Michael O'Laughlin, probably as a result of a tip from someone to whom he had bragged about his friendship with Booth.

Shortly before 11:30 p.m. on that busy Monday, the authorities again descended on Mary Surratt's boardinghouse and arrested everyone there. Those apprehended were Mrs. Surratt, her daughter, her niece and a teen-age boarder. While the women were gathering their belongings, an astonishing interruption took place. The doorbell rang and the officers were confronted by a big, muscular man, his boots covered with mud, a woolen cap pulled low on his head and a pickax resting on his shoulder. The stranger claimed that he had been hired by Mrs. Surratt to dig a gutter, to which she replied, "Before God, I do not know this man, and have never seen him before, and I did not hire him to dig a gutter for me." Upon further questioning, the mysterious stranger pulled out a certificate signifying that he had taken an oath of allegiance to the Union. The name on the document was Lewis Paine, which meant absolutely nothing to the police officers.

Paine, it turned out, had spent three days hiding in a wooded lot about a mile from the Navy Yard Bridge before seeking refuge at Mrs. Surratt's boardinghouse. He was hauled off to Augur's headquarters on general suspicion, and within a few hours he was identified by William Seward's servant, William Bell, as the man who had so savagely attacked the Secretary of State. Meanwhile, Mary Surratt was placed in a cell in the Carroll Annex of the Old Capitol Prison — where another woman prisoner, kept directly below, heard the sound of "Mrs. Surratt's

little feet, walking up and down, up and down all through the night."

Three days later, on Thursday, April 20, George Atzerodt was arrested. After leaving Pennsylvania House early on the morning after Lincoln's assassination, Atzerodt had made his way on foot and by stage to the home of a cousin, Hartman Richter, who lived near Germantown, Maryland. There he had stayed quietly, sometimes emerging to tend the garden. On April 19, the authorities had received a tip that a strange character was lurking about the Richter place. Further information had come from Atzerodt's own brother, who was a deputy on the staff of the provost marshal of Baltimore. When John Atzerodt heard that government authorities were looking for his brother George, he suggested the Richter house as a likely place for George to hide.

The army sergeant sent to arrest the fugitive did not find Richter's house until near daybreak on the 20th. As it happened, Atzerodt had gone to bed drunk and was sleeping it off when the sergeant rudely wakened him. He went without a word of protest, as if he had expected all along that only the worst could happen to George Atzerodt.

Finally, on April 24, came the official rap on the door of Dr. Samuel Mudd. The authorities had been slow in getting to Mudd partly out of ineptitude and partly because they were unsure about the extent of his involvement. The story Mudd told them was that although he had not recognized Booth when setting his leg, he had begun to get suspicious almost as soon as the injured man left the Mudd farmstead. During his brief trip to Bryantown, said the doctor, he had heard about the assassination from troopers of the 13th New York Cavalry, who were

Lewis Paine, disguised as a laborer, arrives at the door of Mary Surratt's boardinghouse and is confronted by investigators who have come to arrest all of the residents. Taken into custody, Paine later said he bitterly regretted having incriminated Mrs. Surratt by returning to her house.

Hartman Richter lights the way as arresting officers awaken his cousin, George Atzerodt, from a drunken slumber in Richter's home. During the trial that followed, Atzerodt's defense hinged on his reputation for cowardice; his lawyer argued that even if Atzerodt had been assigned to assassinate the Vice President, "he never could have done it."

scouring the countryside. Returning to his farm, he had found Booth and Herold riding off into the Zekiah Swamp.

His immediate impulse, Mudd said, had been to go back to Bryantown and alert the cavalry; what had restrained him was a fear of reprisals from Confederate sympathizers. The next day, Easter, he had been pondering the problem at church when he had encountered a cousin, Dr. George Mudd, and told him the whole story. George, a staunch Unionist, had agreed to pass the information to Federal officers in Bryantown.

By telling his cousin, Samuel Mudd may have been simply creating a shrewd diversion; the act both demonstrated his good faith and gave John Wilkes Booth time to get away. The federal authorities ruminated about Dr. Mudd's story for nine days — and then arrested him. Excluding Surratt, only Booth and Herold now remained at large.

In his lair near the home of Thomas Jones, Booth whiled away the wretched hours by reading newspaper accounts of the assassination and pursuit, and by scrawling diary entries in a small leather notebook. His mood swung from arrogance to despair. He had "too great a soul to die like a criminal," Booth wrote at one point, and at another he complained bitterly of "being hunted like a dog through swamps and woods," with "every man's hand" against him.

Jones kept the fugitives supplied with food, brandy and papers; he also proved to be steadfastly supportive. During a visit to a bar in Port Tobacco, Jones was approached by a Federal detective who said he would give $100,000 for information leading to Booth's capture. Despite the fact that he had invested everything he owned in Confeder-

111

ate bonds, which were now worthless, Jones barely blinked. "That's a large sum of money," he said. "It ought to get him if money can do it." Then he returned to his drink.

On April 20, Jones heard that Federal cavalry in the vicinity was being moved to St. Mary's County, where Booth reportedly had been seen. It seemed time for Booth and Herold to try crossing the Potomac into Virginia. That night, Jones went to the thicket and told Booth and Herold that it was clear.

With Booth mounted on Jones's horse and Herold leading it, the three men moved cautiously out of the underbrush, down the public road and across fields toward the Potomac. Jones scouted ahead, pausing to give a low whistle as a signal that all was well. He had a boat hidden close to the river, back in a tributary stream. Although the grateful Booth wanted to reward him generously,

Jones would accept only $18, the price he had paid for the boat. Booth seated himself in the stern, while Herold manned the oars. Thomas Jones stood on the shore listening until he could no longer hear the creak of the oarlocks sounding across the water.

For the rest of the night, David Herold rowed and rowed on the serpentine river, to find out at daybreak that not only had the incoming tide carried them several miles upstream, but that they were also still on the Maryland side. Recognizing the terrain, Herold put ashore and made his way to the farm of Peregrine Davis, a known Confederate supporter; he obtained provisions from Davis' son-in-law, John J. Hughes. The two fugitives lay hidden near the Davis farm on Friday and Saturday.

By now the countryside was swarming with pursuers. Many military units and civil-

David Herold rows Booth and himself out onto the misty, two-mile-wide Potomac River toward Virginia on the night of April 20. The former Confederate agent who provided the boat noted that Booth's injured leg was worsening and that the assassin had become "a cripple, to whom every step was torture."

The escape route of Booth and Herold runs southeast from Washington into Maryland, swings around Bryantown, and then turns southwest through a sparsely settled region to the Potomac River. Once in Virginia the fugitives crossed the Rappahannock on the ferry at Port Conway; they holed up about two miles farther on, at the Garrett farm.

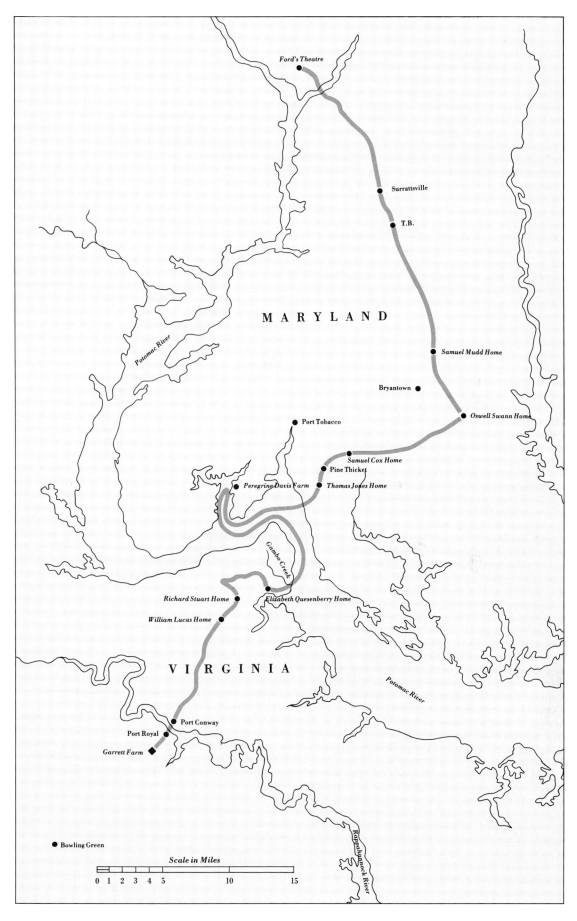

Ford's Theatre

Surrattsville

T.B.

MARYLAND

Potomac River

Samuel Mudd Home

Bryantown

Oswell Swann Home

Port Tobacco

Samuel Cox Home

Pine Thicket

Peregrine Davis Farm

Thomas Jones Home

Gambo Creek

Richard Stuart Home

Elizabeth Quesenberry Home

William Lucas Home

VIRGINIA

Potomac River

Port Conway

Port Royal

Garrett Farm

Bowling Green

Rappahannock River

Scale in Miles

0 1 2 3 4 5   10   15

ian posses were in the field, all of them eager to lay their hands on rewards that eventually totaled $200,000. Because of jealousy, greed and ambition, there was little cooperation among the various groups—and almost no sharing of information. General Augur, commander of the Department of Washington, learned as early as April 21 or 22, for example, that Booth had broken his leg and had been treated by Dr. Mudd—but Augur failed at first to pass on this information to the War Department.

Prominent among the pursuers were Major James R. O'Beirne, provost marshal for the Department of Washington, who headed a squad of detectives; and Colonel Lafayette C. Baker, head of the War Department's secret police and one of the Civil War's least savory figures. Baker, though an able organizer, was a notoriously venal man whose department was full of corruption. But Stanton had faith in Baker; according to Baker, the Secretary of War had assured him that "my whole dependence is upon you."

Yet it was O'Beirne rather than Baker who was most closely on the fugitives' trail when they again attempted to cross the Potomac on Saturday night, April 22. O'Beirne had found a farm girl near the Zekiah Swamp who had seen two men, one using a crutch, emerge from the woods and ask for food. O'Beirne's detectives immediately started scouring the area, finding crutch marks but not the fugitives. Booth and Herold had made it across the Potomac River on their second try—they landed at Gambo Creek—probably without realizing how hotly they were being hunted.

At long last John Wilkes Booth had made good his flight to the Confederacy for which, in the words of his diary, he had "given up all

that was holy and sweet." Yet his welcome was far from enthusiastic. Virginia was by then, of course, occupied by Federal troops. Rare indeed was the Southern loyalist courageous or foolhardy enough to provide haven for the assassin of Abraham Lincoln.

The fugitives therefore found themselves being shunted from one place to another by Virginians who consented to give them food but were unwilling to take them into their homes. Their first stop was the cottage of a Mrs. Elizabeth Quesenberry, who gingerly passed them along to the summer home of Dr. Richard Stuart. Stuart, who had been active in the Confederate underground, al-

William Jett, an 18-year-old Confederate cavalry veteran returning home after his unit's surrender, found refuge for Booth and Herold at the farm of his friend Richard Garrett. Never brought to trial for aiding the fugitives, Jett was a tobacco salesman in Baltimore when he sat for the photograph above, eight years later. He eventually died in an asylum, still chastising himself for the trouble he had brought to Garrett.

The Star Hotel in Bowling Green, Virginia, operated by the Gouldman family, had been a haven for Confederate agents during the War. For Willie Jett, in the spring of 1865, it was the home of his sweetheart, 16-year-old Izora Gouldman; their courtship ended after the Booth episode.

lowed the scruffy-looking travelers to eat in his kitchen; then he directed them to the nearby log cabin of a free black, William Lucas, where they spent the night of April 23. Early the next morning, for the sum of $20, Booth and Herold prevailed on Lucas' son Charlie to conceal them in a wagonload of straw and drive them to the Rappahannock River. They reached the north bank of the river near Port Conway, Virginia, at about 9 o'clock on the morning of April 24.

Finding that the scow that served as a ferry was on the opposite shore, they tried to get a local resident, William Rollins, to row them across. He declined. But the appearance of the two strangers interested Rollins' wife, Bettie, whose critical observations would prove extremely valuable to the men who were searching for Booth. Since the fugitives were without horses, they had no choice but to stay put until the ferry came across.

While Booth and Herold waited impatiently, three ex-Confederate soldiers — William S. Jett of the 9th Virginia Cavalry and Absalom R. Bainbridge and Mortimer B. Ruggles, both of John S. Mosby's guerrillas — rode up to the ferry slip. At first Herold told them that his name was Boyd and that the crippled man was his brother, James W. Boyd. Booth's alias may have been chosen because it accorded with the initials JWB that he, as a boy, had tattooed on the back of his left hand.

Herold suggested to the Confederates that if they were "raising a command to go South," he and Booth would like to go with them. When he received evasive replies, he suddenly blurted out in a trembling voice: "We are the assassinators of the President!" By the time Booth came hobbling over, Herold had revealed their true names and asked for assistance. Willie Jett, who did most of the talking, agreed to help get the fugitives across the river and find shelter for them. The ferry came in about noon, and all five men made the 300-yard crossing to Port Royal, on the southern shore.

With Booth mounted on Ruggles' horse and the others doubling up, the group rode up the steep incline from the ferry slip and stopped a few hundred feet away, at the home of Randolph Peyton, a friend of Willie Jett's. In Peyton's absence, his two maiden sisters provided the unexpected guests with refreshments in the parlor. Passing himself off as a returning Confederate soldier, Booth was at his most charming. Nonetheless, the sisters hesitated to provide refuge to the stranger, since they were alone in the house.

It mattered little. Only three miles down the road, toward Bowling Green, was the farm of Richard Garrett, whom Jett knew to be unswervingly loyal to the Confederacy. Sure enough, when Jett and Booth knocked on Garrett's door and assured him that "Boyd" was a Confederate soldier who had been wounded at Petersburg, the farmer of-

Message from an Anguished Brother

Handsome and pensive, acclaimed as the finest actor on the American stage, Edwin Booth doted on his daughter Edwina.

Edwin Booth was still mourning the 1863 death of his actress-wife, Mary Devlin, when the appalling deed of his brother John Wilkes struck him another blow. Edwin expressed his anguish in an open letter (below), vowing never to perform again. When debt drove him back to the stage in less than a year, his public rejoiced.

To the people of the United States.
My fellow citizens:

When a nation is overwhelmed with sorrow by a great public calamity, the mention of private grief would under ordinary circumstances be an intrusion, but under those by which I am surrounded, I feel sure that a word from me will not be so regarded by you.

It has pleased God to lay at the door of my afflicted family the life-blood of our great, good and martyred President. Prostrated to the very earth by this dreadful event, I am yet but too sensible that other mourners fill the land. To them, to you, one and all go forth our deep, unutterable sympathy; our abhorrence and detestation of this most foul and atrocious of crimes.

For my mother and sisters, for my two remaining brothers and my own poor self, there is nothing to be said except that we are thus placed without any agency of our own. For our loyalty as dutiful, though humble, citizens, as well as for our consistent, and as we had some reason to believe, successful, efforts to elevate our name, personally and professionally, we appeal to the record of the past. For our present position we are not responsible. For the future — alas! I shall struggle on, in my retirement, with a heavy heart, an oppressed memory and a wounded name — dreadful burdens — to my too welcome grave.

Your afflicted friend,

Edwin Booth

NEW YORK, APRIL 20, 1865

fered Booth a bed for the night. Their primary mission accomplished, Jett, the two other soldiers and Herold rode off toward Bowling Green, 10 miles away. There, by happy circumstance, the father of Jett's sweetheart owned a local hostelry called the Star Hotel.

Surrounded by the hospitable Garretts, Booth was more comfortable than he had been at any time during his flight. In notes written seven years later, Richard Garrett recalled that Booth sat silently through supper and retired early to a bedroom that he shared with two of Garrett's older sons and two small children. At breakfast Booth seemed refreshed. The younger children accompanied him to the lawn, where he passed most of the morning reclining beneath a locust tree. In the meantime, the eldest of Garrett's sons rode to a shoemaker, about a mile away, seeking new footwear for Booth. While there he saw a newspaper announcing a large reward for Booth's capture. When Booth heard about it, he remarked coolly that he was surprised the reward was not even larger. In his opinion, he told one of Garrett's daughters, the assassination would ultimately benefit the South — for there was bound to be revolution on the accession of the hard-drinking Andrew Johnson.

After lunch with the family, Booth went out on the porch, where Ruggles, Bainbridge and David Herold found him when they returned to the farm at about three in the afternoon. Anxious to resume their journey home, Ruggles and Bainbridge had left Willie Jett with his sweetheart back at the Star Hotel. They introduced Herold as "Boyd's" younger brother Davey. Then, after saying good-by to Booth and Herold, they swung into their saddles and rode out of the farmyard, heading for the ferry at Port Royal.

Before long, however, the two Confederates were back with alarming news: Federal cavalry had crossed the Rappahannock at Port Royal and were even now coming down the road toward the Garrett farm. "You must take care of yourselves the best way you can," Richard Garrett remembered the soldiers calling out to Booth and Herold before wheeling their horses and galloping away.

The Grieving Nation's Long Farewell

THE NATION MOURNS

A

MARTYRED

FATHER!

LOAG, Printer, Fourth & Chestnut.

Abraham Lincoln's death triggered an outpouring of grief beyond anything the United States had ever known. Within an hour after the President's body had been removed to the White House, all of Washington was shrouded in black. "It seemed," said one citizen, "as if the whole world had lost a dear, personal friend."

On the 18th of April, 25,000 people filed sorrowfully through the White House, where Lincoln lay in state. The next noon, funeral services were held in the East Room *(right)*, and all over the nation Americans thronged to their local churches.

From the White House, Lincoln's body was taken under escort to the Capitol Rotunda. Minute guns boomed, church bells tolled, bands played dirges, and 40,000 mourners followed the hearse as it made its way up Pennsylvania Avenue.

On April 21, a special train carrying Lincoln and the disinterred remains of his son Willie, who had died in 1862 at the age of 12, began the journey back to Illinois. Each city along the train's 1,700-mile run held its own public salute. "The intensity of feeling seemed to grow deeper," said one of the entourage accompanying Lincoln's body, "as the President's remains went further westward." By May 4, when Lincoln was entombed near his Springfield home, more than seven million people had shared in the emotional good-by.

EAST.

Admit the Bearer to the
EXECUTIVE MANSION,
On WEDNESDAY, *the*
19th of April, 1865.

This pass was required for admission to the White House funeral ceremony *(right)*. Distribution was limited to senior government and military officials, foreign representatives and notable citizens.

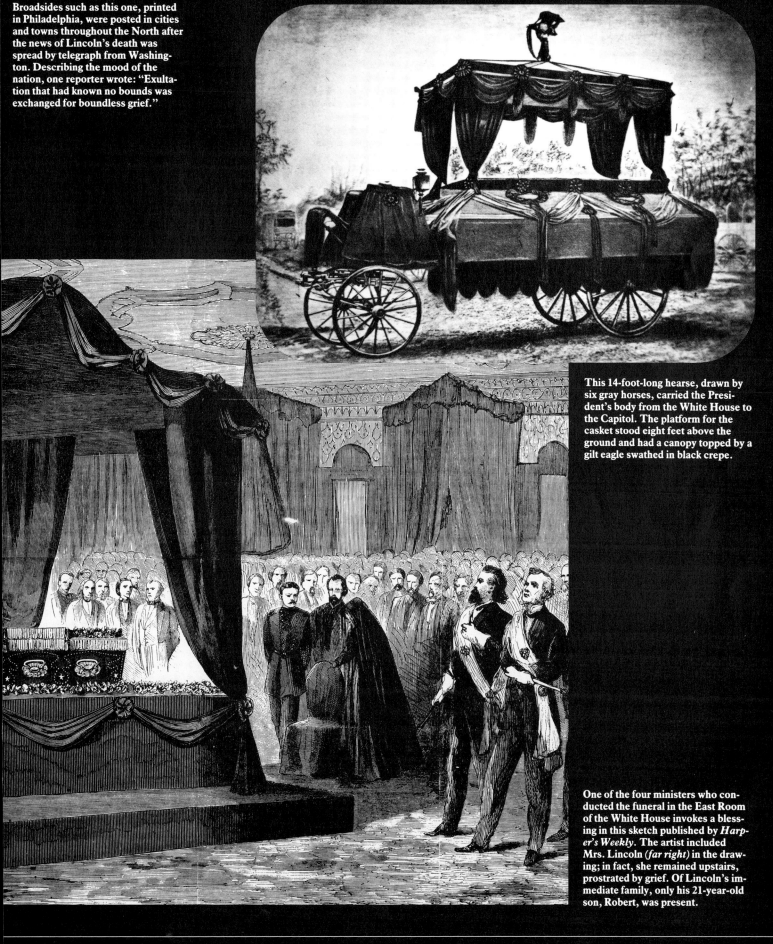

Broadsides such as this one, printed in Philadelphia, were posted in cities and towns throughout the North after the news of Lincoln's death was spread by telegraph from Washington. Describing the mood of the nation, one reporter wrote: "Exultation that had known no bounds was exchanged for boundless grief."

This 14-foot-long hearse, drawn by six gray horses, carried the President's body from the White House to the Capitol. The platform for the casket stood eight feet above the ground and had a canopy topped by a gilt eagle swathed in black crepe.

One of the four ministers who conducted the funeral in the East Room of the White House invokes a blessing in this sketch published by *Harper's Weekly*. The artist included Mrs. Lincoln (*far right*) in the drawing; in fact, she remained upstairs, prostrated by grief. Of Lincoln's immediate family, only his 21-year-old son, Robert, was present.

Honors on a Solemn Journey

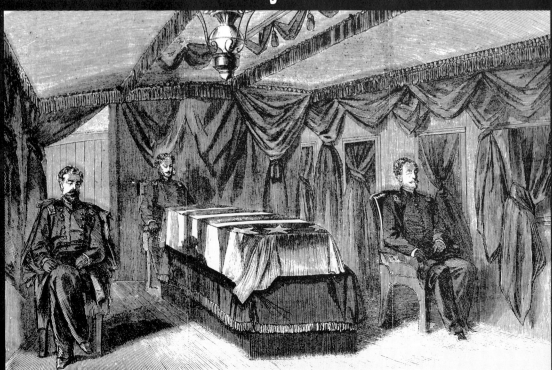

Heading northeast on its way out of Washington, the funeral train makes one of its first stops in Philadelphia. The car carrying Lincoln and his son Willie is second from the end; the locomotive and other cars were changed periodically so that various railroad companies might be given the opportunity to participate.

An ornate hearse that was built for the occasion carries Lincoln's casket up Broad Street in Philadelphia. Several people were injured in the rush to view the President's body at historic Independence Hall.

A ferry transports the presidential railroad car across the Hudson River, from New Jersey to New York City. Lincoln's casket had been removed from the car at Jersey City and was sent over on a separate boat.

Broadway's Heartfelt Regards

Soldiers with reversed arms accompany the huge canopied hearse built for Lincoln by a New York undertaker, Peter Relyea. Each of the 16 horses pulling the hearse wore a black plume and blanket; each pair of horses was led by a groom in a top hat.

The Lincoln cortege, comprising 75,000 civilians and 11,000 men in uniform, moves slowly up Broadway on April 25, 1865. "New York never before saw such a day," wrote one observer. "Rome in the palmiest days of its power never witnessed such a triumphal march."

Spectators perch in trees and wait on rooftops for a view of the march from New York's City Hall to the station of the Hudson River Railroad, which took 3 hours 48 minutes. More than one million people — an extraordinary figure for the time — watched the funeral procession.

In the sole photograph of Lincoln after his death, the President lies in the rotunda of New York's City Hall. Behind the casket, a decoration from which is shown above, are busts of Daniel Webster (left) and Andrew Jackson. Rear Admiral Charles H. Davis, representing the Navy, stands at the President's head; Brigadier General Edward D. Townsend, representing the Army, stands at his feet. Townsend's decision to allow photographer Jeremiah Gurney to take pictures of the corpse infuriated Gurney's competitors and outraged Mary and Robert Lincoln, who considered it bad taste. Secretary of War Stanton subsequently ordered Gurney's plates and prints destroyed; only this print, which Gurney sent to Stanton in a desperate effort to save his work, survived.

A Stately Passage Westward

Lincoln's hearse is engulfed by mourners in Buffalo. Former President Millard Fillmore and President-to-be Grover Cleveland paid tribute to Lincoln at this stop.

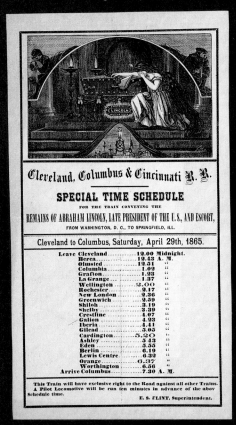

Cleveland, Columbus & Cincinnati R.R.

SPECIAL TIME SCHEDULE

FOR THE TRAIN CONVEYING THE

REMAINS OF ABRAHAM LINCOLN, LATE PRESIDENT OF THE U.S., AND ESCORT,

FROM WASHINGTON, D. C., TO SPRINGFIELD, ILL.

Cleveland to Columbus, Saturday, April 29th, 1865.

Leave Cleveland	12.00 Midnight.
Berea	12.43 A. M.
Olmsted	12.51 "
Columbia	1.02 "
Grafton	1.23 "
La Grange	1.37 "
Wellington	2.00 "
Rochester	2.17 "
New London	2.36 "
Greenwich	2.59 "
Shiloh	3.19 "
Shelby	3.39 "
Crestline	4.07 "
Galion	4.23 "
Iberia	4.41 "
Gilead	5.05 "
Cardington	5.20 "
Ashley	5.43 "
Eden	5.55 "
Berlin	6.19 "
Lewis Centre	6.32 "
Orange	6.37 "
Worthington	6.56 "
Arrive Columbus	7.30 A. M.

This Train will have exclusive right to the Road against all other Trains. A Pilot Locomotive will be run ten minutes in advance of the above Schedule time.

E. S. FLINT, Superintendent.

Each railroad on Lincoln's route home issued precise schedules like this one, which details an Ohio leg of the journey. Between Erie and Cleveland, the train used the same engine and crew as on Lincoln's inaugural trip four years earlier.

Long lines of grieving citizens wait in the rain to view the President's remains, inside a pagoda on Cleveland's

Along the shores of Lake Michigan a handful of men, women and children observe the President's funeral train as it waits on a trestle after its arrival in Chicago.

Monument Square. The city fathers hastily erected the structure because no available building could accommodate the anticipated crowds.

Chicago's Salute to a Favorite Son

The funeral procession halts at the Cook County courthouse in Chicago, where Lincoln would lie in state. A sign over the courthouse entrance read: "Illinois Clasps

Forming under a huge arch near the lakefront at 12th Street and Michigan Avenue, the procession prepares to march through Chicago. The hearse is attended by pallbearers, an honor guard and 36 schoolgirls in white, each representing a state in the reunited nation.

Her Bosom Her Slain, but Glorified Son."

A NATION MOURNS
The Departed
PATRIOT,
STATESMAN,
And MARTYR.

Born February 12th, 1809.
Died April 15th, 1865.

Symbols of mourning, such as the card and badges shown here, were sold by street vendors all over the country. Almost everyone in the North displayed some emblem of respect, either purchased or homemade.

Home to Springfield

Citizens of Springfield, Illinois, await Lincoln's train. "The city is so crowded," complained one reporter, "that it is impossible to procure lodging in a bar-room or on a pool table."

Because Springfield lacked a proper hearse, this one was lent to the city by the mayor of St. Louis, Missouri. The vehicle, which cost $6,000, was finished in gold, silver and crystal.

The roof, columns and copper dome of the Illinois Statehouse, where Lincoln had tried more than 200 cases as a lawyer, are shrouded in black and white cloth. Not enough black cloth was available, so white was used — over the objections of some who thought the color too cheery.

Dressed in their finest, Lincoln's old friends and neighbors file out of the Statehouse after paying their last respects. One of the mourners placed a wreath of flowers (*above*) on the bier.

At Rest at Last

A delegation of Illinois-ans gathers in front of the Lincoln home on the corner of 8th and Jackson Streets in Springfield. Lincoln had hoped to return here after his second term as President.

Crowds throng the hillside around the receiving vault during the burial service at Springfield's Oak Ridge Cemetery on May 4, 1865, which concluded 20 days of national mourning. "He was canonized as he lay on his bier," declared one observer, "by the irresistible decree of countless millions."

This framed memorial wreath was woven for Dr. William Wallace, the Lincolns' family physician. Its braids are made of hair that had been taken from the tail of Lincoln's horse *(below)* and studded with pearls.

The Reverend Henry Brown, a black minister who had known the Lincolns for years, stands to the left of Old Bob, Lincoln's horse, on the day of Lincoln's interment. Brown led Old Bob in the place of honor behind the hearse on the final walk to the cemetery.

The Harsh Reckoning

5

To John Wilkes Booth it must have seemed that he had been betrayed — or that the Federal cavalrymen coming down the road from Port Royal late on the afternoon of April 25, 1865, were gifted with second sight. In fact, the cavalry happened to be in that place at that time because of two strokes of pure luck.

A little before noon of the previous day, while Booth reclined beneath a locust tree on the Garrett farm, Colonel Lafayette Baker stopped by the War Department office of Secretary Edwin Stanton's assistant, Major Thomas Eckert. Eckert showed Baker a newly arrived telegram declaring that Booth and Herold had been sighted crossing the Potomac near Swan Point on April 16. Although the report was inaccurate — the men observed were actually two Confederate agents named Joseph Baden and Thomas Harbin — it drew attention to the area where Booth and Herold had crossed unseen on April 22. Spurred by the incorrect telegram, Baker set out after the wrong men, but in the right direction.

Baker got authorization from Stanton for a cavalry detail to mount a search in Virginia. The 26 men assigned to the mission were drawn from the headquarters detail of the 16th New York Cavalry, most of whom had been assigned to accompany the Lincoln funeral cortege. Lieutenant Edward P. Doherty was in nominal command, but he was in fact subordinate to two of Baker's detectives: Lieutenant Colonel Everton J.

Conger, a wounded war veteran; and Lieutenant Luther B. Baker, who was Lafayette Baker's cousin.

Loading horses and men on board the steamer *John S. Ide* about midafternoon on April 24, the cavalry contingent proceeded down the Potomac to Belle Plain, near Fredericksburg, Virginia, arriving there about 10 o'clock that night. Next day the troopers rode 11 miles southeast, to the point where the ferry crossed the Rappahannock from Port Conway to Port Royal. There they encountered and questioned William Rollins, who told them that two civilians, one of them crippled, had crossed the Rappahannock the day before, in the company of three Confederate soldiers. The crucial information, however, was provided by Rollins' wife, Bettie. She had recognized one of the Confederate soldiers as Willie Jett: A good place to look for him, she suggested, was at the hotel of his sweetheart's father in Bowling Green.

That information sent the soldiers flying down the road to Bowling Green — and straight past the Garrett farm, where Booth and Herold, upon learning of their pursuers' approach, hid in a stand of pines. Once the sound of hoofbeats died away, the two returned to Garrett's house. "Boyd" explained to Garrett that he had run afoul of Federals in Maryland; he then asked if he and his companion could rent transportation so they could ride the 11 miles to Guinea Station and join a Maryland Confederate artillery unit

The noose above, made from Boston hemp three quarters of an inch thick, was one of four fashioned by the government's executioner, Captain Christian Rath, for use in hanging the conspirators sentenced to death for Lincoln's assassination. On July 7, 1865, Rath adjusted this noose around the neck of Lewis Paine.

that was supposedly nearby. Wary and fearful, Garrett refused. It was too late, he argued — daylight was rapidly fading — but he promised he would furnish transportation in the morning. Not wishing to have the fugitives stay in his house, he agreed to let them spend the night in a barn, once used as a tobacco-drying shed and presently a place for storing old furniture. Concerned that the visitors might try to steal his horse during the night, Garrett instructed his 17-year-old son, John M. (Jack) Garrett, to padlock the barn door from the outside.

Meanwhile, Booth's pursuers were riding hard toward Bowling Green, which was 13 miles from the Garrett farm. Midway there, they stopped at a notorious bawdyhouse known to its patrons as The Trap. The proprietress was a widow named Martha Carter, who had four daughters. To Lieutenant Doherty and Colonel Conger, it seemed a likely stopping place for the Confederate soldiers they were seeking and perhaps for Booth as well. On being questioned, the Carter daughters denied seeing a lame man — but they admitted that three Confederate soldiers and a man answering the description of Herold had been there the day before. Sure that they were now hot on the fugitives' trail, the cavalrymen rode on toward Bowling Green. About midnight they surrounded the Star Hotel, where Willie Jett was sleep-

ing soundly in a room on the second floor.

Taken by surprise before he could get out of bed, Willie talked freely: He conceded that he had left Booth at the Garrett farm and that Herold had returned there that afternoon. By the time they began backtracking to the Garrett farm, the men of the 16th New York were almost asleep in their saddles; they had been on the move continuously for more than 24 hours. Lieutenant Doherty detailed a sergeant by the name of Boston Corbett to the rear of the column to prevent any stragglers from dropping out.

Corbett was himself worth keeping an eye on — indeed, he was one of the more unusual characters in an army well supplied with eccentrics. Born Thomas H. Corbett in London, he had migrated to the United States, married, and worked as a hatter. The death of his wife in childbirth had deranged him. Taking to drink, he had become a derelict — until, one night in Boston, he saw the light of God, in token whereof he adopted the city's name as his own.

From then on, as a street-corner preacher, Corbett heard heavenly voices, consorted with angels and read divine signs in the sky. In 1858, he was solicited by two prostitutes after attending a revival meeting; although he did not succumb, he was apparently at least tempted — whereupon, in remorse, he castrated himself.

Now, pushed to their destination by Sergeant Corbett, the Union cavalrymen and detectives stealthily disposed themselves in the farmyard of Richard Garrett at 2 o'clock on the morning of April 26.

Despite their attempts to be quiet, the Federals aroused Garrett's dogs, whose barking brought the farmer to his front door. Colonel

Conger stuck a pistol in his face and, when Garrett professed ignorance of Booth's whereabouts, ordered a rope placed around his neck, threatening to hang him then and there. Young Jack Garrett intervened: The men they were looking for, he volunteered, were sleeping in the barn.

The barn was surrounded. Lieutenant Doherty yelled for Booth and Herold to come out. There was no reply. Luther Baker took over, shouting that he was going to send Jack Garrett into the barn: Booth and Herold should give him their weapons, then walk out behind him, hands in the air. At Baker's command, Jack Garrett turned a key in the padlock and opened the door. Baker shoved him into the barn, slammed the door and jumped to one side, avoiding possible shots. Inside, Garrett found Booth awake and enraged. "Damn you!" the fugitive growled at him. "You have betrayed me!" Garrett fled the barn empty-handed.

From their positions outside the barn, the Union men could hear an argument within: David Herold wanted desperately to surrender, and Booth was furious. "You're a goddamn coward," he snarled, "and mean to leave me in my distress." To the enemy outside, Booth called, "There is a man in here who wants to surrender awful bad." He added that Herold was "innocent of any crime whatever." The door opened, and Herold stumbled out gabbling protestations of innocence. "If you don't shut up," said an exasperated soldier, "we will cut off your damn head." Subsiding, Herold was tied to a tree.

Again Baker called out to Booth, threatening to burn the barn. Booth pleaded for time to think. Ten or 15 minutes went by; then Baker repeated the threat. Amazingly, Booth responded by proposing a formal combat. "Draw up your men before the door," he called, "and I'll come out and fight the whole command." Baker refused — and Booth showed that he still knew how to play to an audience. "Well, my brave boys," he cried, "prepare a stretcher for me!"

By then Everton Conger had gone around to a corner of the barn. Reaching through a wide crack in the boards, he seized a tuft of hay, set it afire and threw it back into the barn, which "lit right up at once." To soldiers peering through chinks in the barn walls, it seemed that Booth was still planning to fight his way out. Peeking through the door, Luther Baker saw the assassin silhouetted against the dancing flames "with a crutch under each arm and a carbine resting at his hips." According to Baker, Booth dropped one crutch and started toward the fire. He got within six or eight feet of the side of the barn and peered all about "as though he should like to see who fired the barn. Then he seemed to give it up." Turning, Booth dropped his second crutch and began to move toward the door "with a kind of limping, halting jump."

At that moment a shot was fired — and John Wilkes Booth fell in his tracks. Baker and Conger rushed in and dragged out the wounded man. With the help of some troopers, they carried him to Garrett's porch and placed him on a mattress that had been brought from the house.

Although Booth was at last in their hands, Baker and Conger were far from elated: Secretary Stanton, who wished above all else to place the assassin of President Lincoln on public trial, had ordered them to capture Booth, not to kill him. Worried, Conger and Baker began questioning the troopers, each of whom denied firing the shot through a gap

An imaginative period print depicts the fatal confrontation between Lincoln's assassin and soldiers of the 16th New York Cavalry. While conspirator David Herold is taken into custody (far right), Sergeant Boston Corbett takes aim at John Wilkes Booth, seen through a cutaway in the side of the Garrett barn (left).

in the barn's slats — until Sergeant Boston Corbett spoke up and said he was the man responsible. Corbett later stated his reason: He had feared that Booth was about to shoot at one of the officers.

For three and a half hours, Corbett's victim lay bleeding and paralyzed from a bullet that had passed through his neck from the right side to the left, damaging his spinal cord. At one point he muttered to officers kneeling over him: "Tell Mother that I died for my country." Finally, as a shimmering dawn came to the Virginia countryside, John Wilkes Booth asked for his arms to be raised so that he could see his hands.

Looking at them, he murmured, "Useless." And again, "Useless." They were the last words uttered by the man who had killed Abraham Lincoln.

Booth breathed his last a few minutes after 7 o'clock. Lieutenant Doherty ordered that the body be sewn in a saddle blanket with

An engraving published in *Frank Leslie's Illustrated Newspaper* shows Federal soldiers dragging John Wilkes Booth from the burning barn. "There was nothing very grand in his exit," *Leslie's* reported; "Smoked out like a rat and shot like a dog!"

needle and thread obtained from the Garrett house. Then Booth's remains were put on a ramshackle wagon and driven to Belle Plain, where the steamer *John S. Ide* was waiting. Alongside the wagon, guarded by soldiers, his feet tied to his stirrups, rode David Herold. Also under arrest, for having disobeyed orders by killing Booth, was Corbett.

Even before Booth died, Colonel Conger had left the Garrett farm and gone back to Washington. Now, as the *John S. Ide* with Booth's body aboard headed toward Alexandria, Conger and Colonel Lafayette Baker went to report to Edwin Stanton. The Secretary of War was resting on a sofa in his home when Baker burst in exclaiming "We have got Booth!" Stanton put his hands to his eyes and lay for a long moment without saying a word. Then he rose, calmly put on his coat and began to examine some articles that Conger had taken from Booth. They included a holster, a pipe, a compass, a Canadian bill of exchange, a knife, two pistols and Booth's little diary.

Oddly, Stanton did not respond angrily to the news that Booth was mortally wounded.

One reason for his restraint must have been relief. In the 12 days since the assassination, recalled Baker, Stanton had become "very despondent regarding the capture, and had often spoken of the disgrace it would be if the base assassins should escape." Grateful that the ordeal was over, Stanton would soon be hailing Boston Corbett as a hero. "The rebel is dead," Stanton would proclaim. "The patriot lives."

At the moment, however, Stanton's chief thought was of the steamer *John S. Ide*, which was churning up the Potomac. He instructed Baker to meet the boat at Alexandria and to see that David Herold, with Booth's body, was taken by tugboat to the Navy Yard, situated on the Eastern Branch of the Potomac. With Baker in command, the tugboat arrived at the Navy Yard about 2 a.m. on the morning of April 27. There Herold and Booth's corpse were transferred to the monitor *Montauk*, where Herold was imprisoned in the hold. Word spread that the body of the President's assassin lay on the *Montauk's* deck, and a crowd began to gather onshore. For Baker and his men, the first

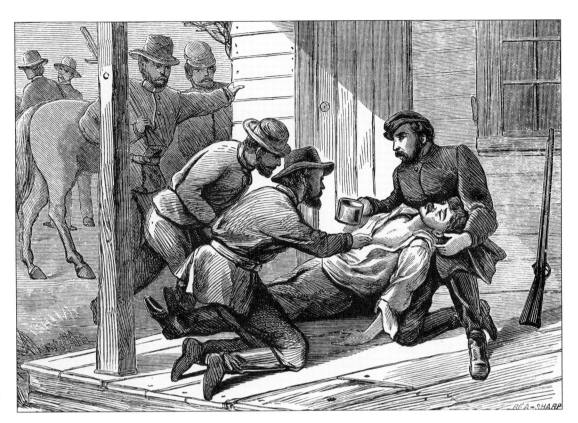

Having carried Booth to the porch of the Garrett house, his captors attempt to revive the dying man with a cup of water. When Booth gasped, "Kill me, kill me," Lieutenant Luther Baker replied, "We don't want to kill you, we want you to get well."

order of business was to establish beyond any reasonable doubt that the dead man was really John Wilkes Booth. It turned out to be no easy task.

In death, the actor who had once preened himself on being America's handsomest man was a hideous sight: He was filthy, his hair was matted, and his emaciated face was darkened by exposure and covered by an 11-day growth of beard. Nonetheless, at least 10 persons, with varying degrees of certainty, identified the corpse as that of John Wilkes Booth. Although the tattooed initials on the body's hand were convincing enough, the firmest evidence came from Booth's dentist — who recognized several fillings in the cadaver's mouth as his own recent handiwork — and from Dr. John Frederick May, who two years earlier had operated to remove a fibroid tumor from the back of Booth's neck. After the surgery, while Booth had been engaged in a strenuous onstage love scene with actress Charlotte Cushman, the wound had torn open. May had tried to repair the damage, but the incident had left a large, easily recognizable scar.

Once the identification had been completed and the body had been laid out on a carpenter's bench beneath an awning, Surgeon General Joseph K. Barnes, who less than a fortnight earlier had attended the deathbed of Booth's victim, presided over the autopsy. Booth had been struck in the right side of his neck, said the subsequent report, "by a conoidal pistol ball, fired at the distance of a few yards, from a cavalry revolver." In its transverse progress, the bullet had perforated Booth's spinal cord and thus had brought on "general paralysis." The actor had died from asphyxiation.

Shortly after the autopsy was completed, a young woman from the throng that had gathered onshore somehow managed to get aboard the *Montauk*. Obviously of zealous Southern sympathies, she snipped a lock of hair from Booth's head. Lafayette Baker, catching her in the act, forcibly relieved her of the memento. Promptly informed of the incident, Secretary Stanton expressed his determination that no one should "secure a trophy" or by any other means make Booth's murderous deed a "subject of rebel rejoic-

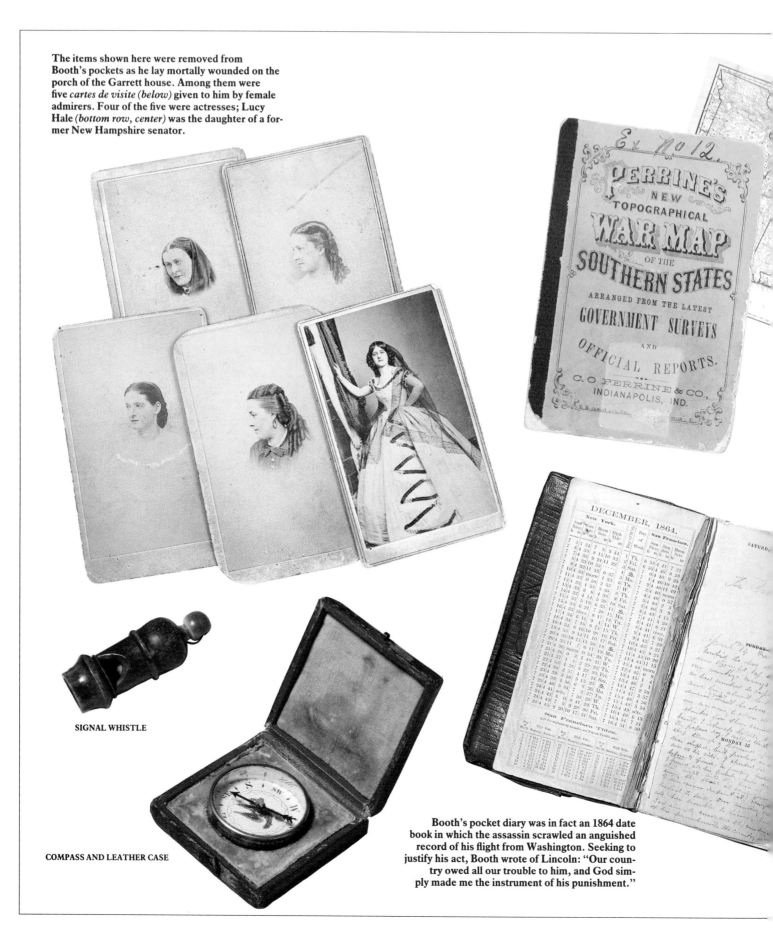

The items shown here were removed from Booth's pockets as he lay mortally wounded on the porch of the Garrett house. Among them were five *cartes de visite (below)* given to him by female admirers. Four of the five were actresses; Lucy Hale *(bottom row, center)* was the daughter of a former New Hampshire senator.

SIGNAL WHISTLE

COMPASS AND LEATHER CASE

Booth's pocket diary was in fact an 1864 date book in which the assassin scrawled an anguished record of his flight from Washington. Seeking to justify his act, Booth wrote of Lincoln: "Our country owed all our trouble to him, and God simply made me the instrument of his punishment."

Booth carried this "War Map of the Southern States." Printed in Indianapolis, the map sold for 50 cents and was accompanied by a 160-page *Handbook of the Rebellion*, a historical record of the recent conflict.

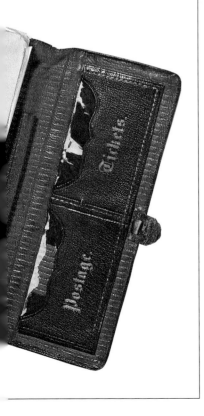

ing." He issued a written order requiring that the corpse be turned over to the custody of Colonel Baker.

That afternoon, Lafayette Baker and his cousin Luther pulled up alongside the *Montauk* in a small boat, manned by two sailors, that carried a heavy iron ball and chain. Taking Booth's body aboard, the group headed down the Eastern Branch toward the Potomac. Baker would later say that at one point he pretended to lower the body into the river, so as to confound the spectators on the distant bank. The boat eventually touched shore at Greenleaf Point — the site of a former federal prison, the Old Penitentiary, which had come to be used as a storage building for the Washington Arsenal.

Night came, and in the darkness Booth's body was carried by soldiers to a large room in the penitentiary. Once an exercise area for inmates, the room was near the west end of the building; it had been personally selected by Stanton, who had carefully studied the penitentiary's floor plans. There, by the light of a single lantern, the soldiers removed bricks from the room's flooring, dug a shallow grave and lowered a wooden rifle case that contained the mortal remains of John Wilkes Booth into the excavation. They covered it with earth and replaced the bricks.

Having disposed of Booth's body, Stanton could turn his full attention to the assassin's accomplices. Kept in the stifling holds of the *Montauk* and its sister ironclad, the *Saugus,* the government's principal male prisoners were manacled with cuffs connected by a stiff iron rod, about 14 inches long, to impede movement of their hands or arms. The shackles around their ankles were linked by chains to 75-pound iron balls.

Stanton, for the ostensible purpose of achieving "better security against conversation," had also commanded that a canvas hood, padded with cotton to a thickness of one inch, with a small hole for eating and breathing but none for seeing or hearing, be placed over the head and laced around the neck of each prisoner. These medieval hoods were worn day and night. As Samuel Arnold wrote later, "Daylight never lit upon the eye, they not even permitting the cap to be withdrawn for the purpose of washing the swollen, bloated and soiled visage."

Presumably on account of her gender, Mary Surratt fared considerably better. Still in the Carroll Annex of the Old Capitol Prison, she was spared the discomfort of a hood; her hands were left free, and only a light chain bound her ankles.

On April 27, under cover of night, the male prisoners were removed from the monitors. Still blinded by their hoods, they were escorted between two ranks of soldiers to cells in the Old Penitentiary, where each was kept under constant watch by two armed soldiers. Stanton's War Department was taking no chances about security: Brigadier General John F. Hartranft, who had been appointed special provost marshal for the arsenal, was assigned a brigade of infantry, a squadron of cavalry and a battery of artillery.

A day or so after the male prisoners had been transferred, Mary Surratt, escorted by Colonel Baker, was conveyed to the arsenal in a closed carriage. She was locked into Cell No. 153, a narrow cubicle that was furnished only with a straw pallet. Later she was given a more spacious and better-equipped room on the third floor.

With the conspirators incarcerated, Stanton moved ahead with plans for their trial.

He proceeded in a fashion that some would call decisive and others rash and impulsive. At least one of Stanton's fellow Cabinet members, Gideon Welles, found his aggressive style "exceedingly repugnant."

First and foremost, the War Secretary, himself an able attorney, was confronted by a question of law. Stanton was inflexible in his resolve that the fate of the defendants be placed in the hands of a military court. His reasoning was simple: In a military court, the laws of evidence were less constricting and the chances of conviction considerably greater than in a civil court. The punishment meted out by military courts also tended to be more severe. Swift and stern punishment of the conspirators was essential, Stanton believed, to prevent a strong resurgence of anti-Southern feeling in the North that could wreck a progressive reconstruction policy.

The problem was that according to long-established doctrine — which, to be sure, had been ignored many times in the course of the war years — civilians could be tried by the military only in places where the civil courts were not functioning. In the District of Columbia, the civil courts had been working without a hitch.

Apparently fretful about the legality of a military trial, Andrew Johnson, the new President, sought an opinion from Attorney General James Speed. The Attorney General responded that if the assassins had acted as "public enemies" of the United States, they "ought to be tried before a military tribunal." He also concluded that they might have violated the laws of war — the accepted rules of conduct for belligerents — and therefore could not be tried before a civil court.

Upon reading Speed's opinion, Edward Bates, who had been Lincoln's first Attorney General, was shocked. Speed, he wrote in his diary, "has been wheedled out of an opinion to the effect that the trial is lawful. If he be, in the lowest degree, qualified for his office, he must know better." Nevertheless, President Johnson issued an order on May 1 requiring that "nine competent military officers" be named to form a commission that would try those accused of complicity in the assassination.

Stanton asked the acting Adjutant General, Edward D. Townsend, to select the officers to serve on the tribunal. Townsend named nine men who had no conflicting assignments; all of them were loyal officers with Republican sympathies. Simplifying the prosecution's task was the fact that the military commission was empowered to formulate its own rules of procedure and to convict by a two-thirds vote rather than by a unanimous decision.

Appointed president of the commission was 62-year-old Major General David Hunter, an officer with a querulous disposition who had been a personal friend of the late President — despite a spotty military record that at one point had led to his removal from command. Although Hunter's strong anti-Southern bias was shared by his colleagues, certain members of the commission would be openly critical of the way he would conduct the trial. Brigadier General August V. Kautz, for example, would object to the favoritism shown to the prosecution, and Colonel Cyrus B. Comstock would doubt the legality of a military panel. Comstock was eventually replaced on the commission, but for reasons that were not associated with his liberal attitudes.

As judge advocate for the trial, Stanton chose an old friend, Brigadier General Jo-

Following a wagon bearing the body of John Wilkes Booth, a detachment of cavalry escorts David Herold through Washington's Navy Yard in the early morning of April 27. Both Herold and the slain assassin were taken aboard the monitor *Montauk*, where four of the other conspirators already were confined.

seph Holt, who headed the War Department's Bureau of Military Justice. A Kentucky lawyer of considerable wealth, Holt had been appointed Judge Advocate General of the Army by Lincoln. In that capacity, he had set up military commissions to prosecute political prisoners accused of "disloyal practices" during the War — a procedure that had been widely criticized as despotic and unconstitutional.

Finally, to assist Holt, Stanton selected another longtime friend, Ohio's John A. Bingham, a Radical member of Congress who was a hellfire-and-brimstone lawyer; and Colonel Henry L. Burnett, an army prosecutor who had argued successfully for the death penalty in Western military trials.

In preparing for the trial of the conspirators, Colonel Burnett worked closely with

Stanton. Day after day and night after night the two labored at assembling evidence. Burnett would remember many instances when he departed utterly exhausted from Stanton's office as late as three in the morning — leaving behind the Secretary of War, who was still hunched over his desk.

On May 4, 1865, after a cross-country procession that drew grieving crowds to every stop of the train that bore his body, Abraham Lincoln was buried in Springfield, Illinois. Five days later, on May 9, those accused of plotting his death went on trial. Promptly at 10 a.m., a door opened at the far end of a room 45 by 30 feet, freshly whitewashed for the occasion, on the third floor of the Old Penitentiary — the same building in which Booth lay buried. One by one, with Sam Ar-

Prisoners in Floating Dungeons

With dozens of alleged conspirators snared in the government's dragnet, Secretary of War Stanton decided to hold six of the most important suspects aboard veritable floating fortresses — the ironclads *Saugus (below)* and *Montauk*. Conditions in the ships' stifling holds were far from humane. The prisoners' legs were chained to 75-pound weights, their wrists were handcuffed to a rigid iron bar, and canvas hoods were placed over their heads. On April 27, the hoods were removed long enough for photographer Alexander Gardner to take the striking portraits on these pages.

LEWIS PAINE

DAVID HEROLD

SAMUEL ARNOLD

MICHAEL O'LAUGHLIN

EDMAN SPANGLER

GEORGE ATZERODT

nold leading and Mary Surratt coming last, the prisoners shuffled onto a foot-high platform and sat down behind a wooden railing.

For their appearance in court, the prisoners' hateful hoods had been removed — only to be replaced whenever the conspirators were returned to their cells. The wrists of all the men were manacled. Lewis Paine and George Atzerodt, considered the most dangerous of the lot, were each trailed by two guards carrying the iron balls that were connected to the prisoners' leg irons; the other men wore lighter steel fetters. As they seated themselves on armless chairs, each of the men was sandwiched between soldiers wearing the sky blue uniform of the Veteran Reserve Corps.

Mrs. Surratt's hands remained free. A dispute, still unresolved, would subsequently rage as to whether ankle chains were hidden beneath her long black skirt. Placed on the far left — from the courtroom spectators' perspective — with a short interval between her and the others, Mrs. Surratt was spared the forbidding presence of soldiers posted on either side of her.

Incredibly, as of the moment the military commission convened, the prisoners had not yet been able to procure counsel. To allow them to attend to that legal necessity, the tribunal therefore adjourned. On the next day, although the defendants were still without lawyers, the commission proceeded to accept their pleas of not guilty and to read to them — for the first time — the charges that they faced.

Although the charges were somewhat different for each individual, the defendants in general were accused of having "traitorously" conspired with Jefferson Davis, Jacob Thompson, Clement C. Clay, Beverly Tucker, George N. Sanders, William C. Cleary,

Mary Surratt was one of many suspected conspirators held in Washington's Old Capitol Prison (below), a dilapidated structure that had served as the temporary seat of Congress after the British had burned the U.S. Capitol in 1814. For two years prior to Mrs. Surratt's stay, no inmate had managed to escape from the prison, which was dubbed "the American Bastille."

George Young, George Harper and "others unknown" to "kill and murder" not only President Lincoln, Vice President Johnson and Secretary Seward but also General Ulysses S. Grant. In naming several leading Southerners who were not present, the court was responding to the almost unanimous belief, held by the Northern public and the Administration alike, that the assassination had been the Confederacy's means of continuing the War.

Aside from the imprisoned defendants and Jefferson Davis, the others named were all members or agents of the Confederacy's so-called Canadian Cabinet, a group sent north of the border in 1864 with orders to instigate as much mischief as possible against the United States. None of the Cabinet's schemes — ranging from raids across the border to the planting of fire bombs in New York City — had worked out as planned. And there was no hard proof that the Canadian Cabinet had anything to do with the assassination of President Lincoln.

As it happened, Jefferson Davis had just that morning been captured near Irwinville, Georgia, while trying to reach Confederate forces west of the Mississippi. On the following day, May 11, Clement Clay would voluntarily surrender to Federal authorities. Both were imprisoned in Fort Monroe, Virginia, where they found themselves in a highly anomalous position: Although they had been named as co-conspirators with the members of Booth's group, they had not yet been formally indicted. Yet while Clay and Davis languished in their cells, the prosecution at the Washington Arsenal was presenting evidence against them as if they had been legally charged. In fact, it seemed that along with the conspirators, the entire Confederacy and

all of its adherents were to be placed on trial.

At the arsenal, once the charges were read, the tribunal again adjourned so that the prisoners' families and friends might continue their frantic hunt for attorneys. Given the unpopularity of their cause, the task was a formidable one. Nevertheless, by the 12th of May all of the accused had finally been supplied with legal counsel.

Somewhat surprisingly, the defense attorneys were mostly of a high caliber. Appearing on behalf of Dr. Samuel Mudd and Ned Spangler, for example, was Thomas F. Ewing Jr., brother-in-law of General William Tecumseh Sherman. Ewing had been a strong abolitionist and, in wartime, had been a brigadier general with a reputation for dealing harshly with those he considered to be enemies of the Union.

Representing Paine and Atzerodt was William E. Doster, who had served as Washington's provost marshal, a post in which he had had ample opportunity to observe — and to frown upon — the methods employed by Colonel Lafayette Baker. Samuel Arnold and Michael O'Laughlin found a competent attorney in Walter S. Cox; Frederick Stone, an experienced counselor, accepted David Herold's case "at the earnest request of his widowed mother and estimable sisters."

Overshadowing them all was Reverdy Johnson of Maryland, a grizzled veteran of America's political and legal battles. Blinded in one eye by a ball that had ricocheted while he had been practicing with a dueling pistol, Johnson was said to possess a vocabulary of only 600 words, all of which he used with great eloquence. Long ago, he had resigned as a U.S. senator to serve as Attorney General under President Zachary Taylor; on returning to the Senate, he had been influential

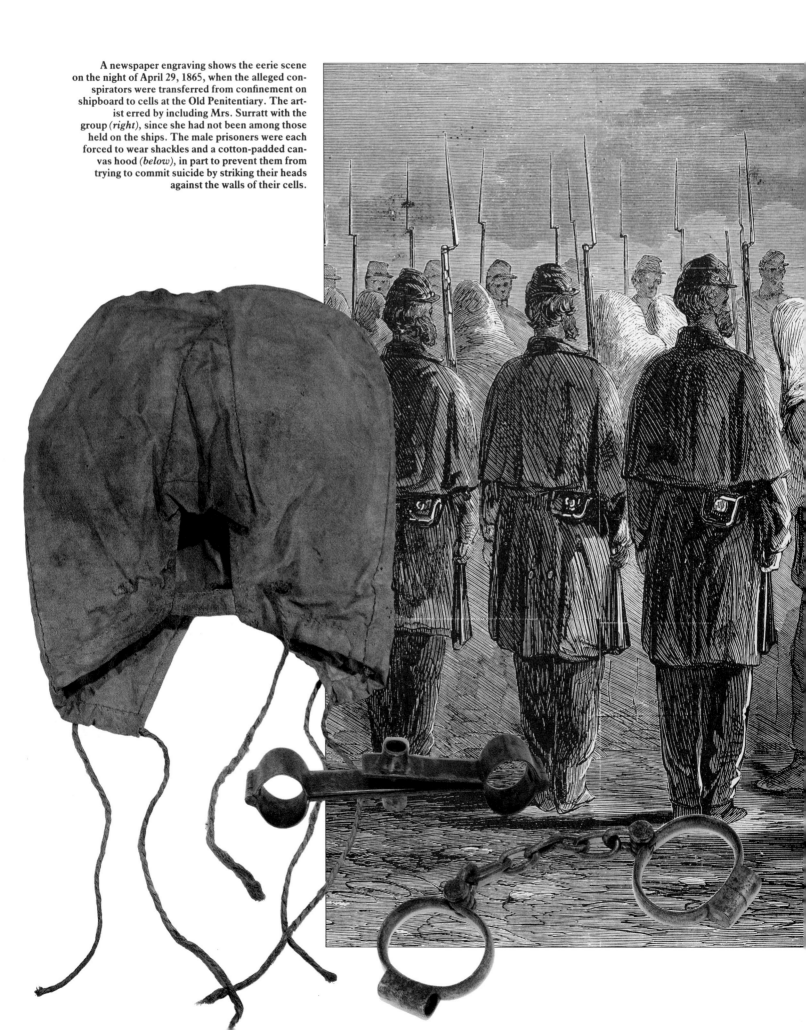

A newspaper engraving shows the eerie scene on the night of April 29, 1865, when the alleged conspirators were transferred from confinement on shipboard to cells at the Old Penitentiary. The artist erred by including Mrs. Surratt with the group (right), since she had not been among those held on the ships. The male prisoners were each forced to wear shackles and a cotton-padded canvas hood (below), in part to prevent them from trying to commit suicide by striking their heads against the walls of their cells.

in keeping Maryland a part of the Union. As a lawyer, Johnson stood at the forefront of the American bar. Although he had never chanced to meet Mary Surratt, he had read of her plight and "deemed it right" that she should not go undefended.

The defense attorneys labored under no delusions. Among the onerous restrictions imposed on them was a ban on letting them talk to the prisoners in their cells. Prisoners who wished to confer with their attorneys could do so only in the crowded courtroom, where the soldiers on each flank could listen in. "This was a contest in which a few lawyers were on one side, and the whole United States on the other," William Doster would remark. To almost everybody, he added, "the verdict was known beforehand."

Yet no one could have foreseen the speed and spite with which the opposition struck. Scarcely had Reverdy Johnson entered the improvised courtroom than General Hunter read an objection raised by Brigadier General Thomas M. Harris, one of the more idiosyncratic members of the commission. A physician in peacetime and an amateur phrenologist, General Harris would later claim that Samuel Mudd "had the bump of secretiveness largely developed. He had the appearance of a natural born liar and deceiver." At the moment, however, Harris' primary concern was Reverdy Johnson, whom he accused of being unable to "recognize the moral obligation of an oath designed as a test of loyalty." Outraged, Johnson replied that he had sworn his allegiance to the Union both as a member of the Senate and as a practitioner before the U.S. Supreme Court. In the wrangling that followed, General Hunter, directing his comments at Johnson, gratuitously announced that the time had passed "when freemen from the North were to be bullied and insulted by the humbug chivalry of the South."

Most members of the commission found the attack on Johnson "ill advised," in General Kautz's cautious words—and General Harris ultimately withdrew his objection. But the damage had been done: Reckoning that his continued presence might harm Mary Surratt's case more than it would help, Reverdy Johnson all but withdrew. During the remainder of the trial, he would make only two brief appearances. For the most part he left Mrs. Surratt's fate in the hands of two junior lawyers from his office, Frederick Aiken and John Clampitt. Both men were in their twenties and both were trying their first major case.

Before the newly appointed defense lawyers had a chance to confer with their clients or to examine the case against them, a parade of 198 prosecution witnesses began. Of these, 68 would testify to sins of the Confederacy—mistreatment of Yankee prisoners, for example—not even remotely connected with the charges against the defendants.

In the calling of witnesses, the defense was at a distinct disadvantage. According to an arbitrary rule of procedure adopted by the court, the defense attorneys were required to provide the Judge Advocate General in advance with a list of the witnesses they intended to call. Since the prosecuting attorneys were under no such constraint, they repeatedly were able to produce surprise witnesses who appeared out of nowhere, gave their sworn testimony and then, as far as the defense lawyers were concerned, vanished. Time and again the prosecution used such witnesses to show that the assassination was part of a Confederate conspiracy.

The first surprise witness was among the first witnesses called. Henry Von Steinacker, as he identified himself, claimed to have been a Confederate topographical officer. In the summer of 1863, said Von Steinacker, he had been riding through Virginia's Shenandoah Valley when he was joined on the road by three strangers. One of them had turned out to be none other than John Wilkes Booth. As they had ridden along together, they had talked about the future of the War. According to Von Steinacker, Booth had stated, "If we only act our part, the Confederacy will gain its independence. Old Abe Lincoln must go up the spout."

Later, Von Steinacker continued, Booth had attended a meeting of Confederate officers in the camp of the 2nd Virginia Infantry Regiment. Although Von Steinacker had not been present, he was later informed that the purpose of the conclave had been to plan Lincoln's assassination.

Caught off-balance, the defense attorneys allowed Von Steinacker to go on his way without cross-examination. During the next fortnight, however, Mrs. Surratt's lawyers came up with some interesting facts about the government's witness, and John Clampitt asked that Von Steinacker be re-called. If the request were granted, he said, he would offer proof that Von Steinacker had originally belonged to the Union Army. Arrested while attempting to desert, he had been sentenced to death but had made an escape while awaiting execution. He had then joined Major General Edward John-

The officers appointed to the military court that tried the conspirators were a mixed lot. Some, like Henry Burnett and James Ekin, had seen little active service, and the records of others were at best uneven. But several had distinguished themselves in battle: Lew Wallace was credited with saving the city of Washington from capture in 1864, Robert Foster had fought gallantly at the siege of Petersburg and Charles Tompkins would eventually be given the Medal of Honor for heroism.

GENERAL THOMAS M. HARRIS   GENERAL LEW WALLACE   GENERAL AUGUST V. KAUTZ   COLONEL HENRY L. BURNETT

COLONEL CHARLES TOMPKINS   COLONEL JAMES A. EKIN   GENERAL ROBERT S. FOSTER   GENERAL JOSEPH HOLT

COLONEL DAVID R. CLENDENIN   GENERAL ALBION P. HOWE   GENERAL DAVID HUNTER   CONGRESSMAN JOHN BINGHAM

son's Confederate force as a draftsman assigned to headquarters, not as an officer. Once again he had gotten into trouble — this time he was convicted of theft and abuse of prisoners — and once again had escaped before he could be punished.

For challenging Von Steinacker's testimony, Clampitt was denounced by a member of the military commission, Major General Lew Wallace, who declared that he held the defense attorney's effort in "supreme contempt." The Judge Advocate General, Joseph Holt, said that he would be happy to have Von Steinacker returned to the courtroom — if only the man could be found. It was later learned that the elusive witness had been a Federal prisoner named Hans Von Winkelstein, who was serving three years for desertion. He had been released immediately after delivering his testimony.

Certain other government witnesses gave their testimony in secret, in a courtroom free of public, press or embarrassing cross-examination. Among them was Richard Montgomery, who admitted to being a double agent in the service of both the Confederates in Canada and the U.S. government. In January of 1865, said Montgomery, Confederate agent Jacob Thompson had told him in Canada about a proposal "to rid the world of the tyrant Lincoln, Stanton, Grant and some others." Subsequently, Montgomery continued, he had been informed that the actor John Wilkes Booth was involved in the assassination plot. Montgomery insisted that he had seen Booth and Booth's henchman, Lewis Paine, in the vicinity of the Confederates' headquarters in Montreal.

Following Montgomery came James B. Merritt, who identified himself as a physician of American parentage now residing in Canada, where he had ingratiated himself with Confederate circles. Merritt told of a similar plot to murder Lincoln, Andrew Johnson and Seward. Mentioned as participants in the scheme, said Merritt, were Booth, John Surratt and someone called "Plug Tobacco" — presumably a reference to Atzerodt, who was nicknamed "Port Tobacco" after his hometown. Merritt also indicated that David Herold was someone he had seen in Canada.

And then there was Sanford Conover, who was perhaps the most convincing witness of the lot. As a roving correspondent for the New York *Tribune,* said Conover, he had gone to Canada and become "quite intimately associated" with various Southern leaders, who had discussed an assassination plot "about as commonly as one would talk of the weather." Conover had seen John Wilkes Booth "strutting about there, dissipating, playing billiards, etc." More than that, Conover said he had seen John Surratt at a meeting given over to a discussion of dispatches from Jefferson Davis and Judah P. Benjamin, the Confederacy's Secretary of State, approving the murders of Lincoln, Johnson, Seward, Stanton, Chief Justice Salmon P. Chase and General Grant.

Not until months after the conspiracy trial was concluded — and its sentences carried out — did the truth about the secret witnesses begin to emerge. Richard Montgomery, whose real name was James Thompson, was exposed as a New York burglar with a long criminal record. James Merritt was brought before a committee of the House of Representatives, where he admitted that his testimony in the conspiracy trial was a tissue of lies — for which the U.S. government had paid him $6,000. As for Sanford Conover, it

This heavy iron key, shown at one half its actual size, was used to lock Mary Surratt in her cell at the Old Penitentiary. Mrs. Surratt and her fellow prisoners were held in alternate cells, to prevent them from communicating with one another.

turned out that his name was Charles A. Dunham and that his testimony had been completely fabricated. Eventually, Conover would be convicted of perjury and sentenced to 10 years in a federal prison.

By that time, unfortunately, the prisoners in the dock of the Washington Arsenal had long since been overtaken by their unhappy destinies.

Of the defendants, three seemed doomed from the start. Several members of Secretary Seward's household told of Paine's wild assault. Atzerodt's well-established lurking about Andrew Johnson's hotel, along with the items found in his room, made him a suitable candidate for the scaffold; David Herold had, after all, accompanied Booth in his flight. Their attorneys did the best they could with what little they had. Herold was portrayed by Frederick Stone as being too simple-minded to know what he was doing; William Doster depicted Atzerodt as so craven that he could not have brought himself to participate in an assassination. Doster had a somewhat more substantial defense for Paine. Unfortunately, in attempting to prove his client insane, Doster received little help from his star medical witness, Dr. Charles H. Nichols, who was the superintendent of Washington's mental hospital.

Asked if Paine's cries of "I'm mad!" as he fled from the Seward home were not evidence of lunacy, Nichols replied, "Such an exclamation would give rise, in my mind, to an impression that the man was feigning insanity." Despite that devastating answer, Doster persisted. Paine had suffered from "long-continued constipation" since his imprisonment, and his lawyer wanted to know if this was not a sign of insanity. Said Dr.

Nichols, "Constipation is not very frequent among the actual insane."

By contrast, the government's case against Ned Spangler was woefully weak. Much was made of a length of rope found in his valise, but several witnesses testified that it might well have been part of the equipment Spangler used when crab-fishing. In addition, stagehand Jacob Ritterspaugh told of following Booth out the rear door of Ford's Theatre but failing to catch him. When he had returned to the stage, said Ritterspaugh, Spangler hit him and warned him not to tell which way Booth had gone: "I asked him what he meant by slapping me in the mouth, and he said, 'For God's sake, shut up'; and that was the last he said."

According to Ritterspaugh's own testimony, there had been a crowd onstage when Spangler slapped him, and an actress named Jenny — presumably Jenny Gourley — was only three or four feet away. Yet the actress was never called as a witness for the prosecution, and Ritterspaugh's testimony remained entirely unsubstantiated.

The cases of Samuel Arnold and Michael O'Laughlin were more complicated. It is a cardinal principle of American law that defendants can only be convicted of the specific crimes with which they have been charged. Sam and Michael, the ne'er-do-wells from the Baltimore area, had undeniably been involved in the earlier conspiracy to abduct President Lincoln.

There was ample evidence to show, however, that Arnold and O'Laughlin had withdrawn from their association with Booth weeks before he had conceived his last-minute attempt on the President's life. For a fortnight before the assassination, Arnold had been working at Fort Monroe, more

A newspaper engraving accurately records the scene in the courtroom where the eight accused conspirators were tried. The prisoners sit in the dock along the rear wall, while the officers comprising the military commission occupy the table at right. The table in the center of the courtroom was reserved for members of the press, and some spectators were seated at the left side of the room. No one was admitted to the court without a pass from the War Department.

than 100 miles from Washington, and numerous witnesses testified to having seen O'Laughlin, unforgettable in his gaudy garb, as he barhopped on the nights of both April 13 and 14. In the end, the prosecution simply decided to ignore the distinction between abduction and assassination. The government lawyers argued that both men had served in the Confederate Army as volunteers and that this attested to a desire on their part to assassinate anyone connected with the U.S. government.

Of all the defendants' cases, Samuel Mudd's was the most time-consuming: Against 23 prosecution witnesses, the defense presented 79. As witness after witness testified to Dr. Mudd's intimacy with Booth, his sympathy for the South, his willingness to hide fugitive Confederates, and his loose talk about the assassination of Lincoln and the President's entire Cabinet, it seemed certain that the doctor would hang. But the defense was able to show that many of the witnesses against Mudd were unreliable and their testimony contradictory or plainly wrong. The single most valuable witness for the defense was the accused's cousin Dr. George Mudd, who testified that the defendant had decided on his own initiative to alert authorities to the odd behavior of the man whose leg he had set. Could he have failed to recognize his illustrious patient, after admittedly encountering him on at least two previous occasions? That, finally, came to be the question on which the court would base its decision.

Because of the spectacular nature of the crime with which the defendants had been charged, it was only natural that passes to the trial should become the most sought-after tickets in town. Wrote an attending newsman: "Major-generals' wives in rustling silks, daughters of congressmen attired like the lilies of the milliner, little girls who hope to be young ladies and have come up with 'Pa' to look at the assassins; even brides are here, in the fresh blush of their nuptuals. They chatter and smile and go up the three flights of stairs to the court-room."

Once admitted, the spectators closely scrutinized the row of prisoners for indications of repentance or guilt. It was noted that O'Laughlin gave signs of anxious remorse and that Arnold kept leaning forward and back while restlessly clasping and unclasping his hands. Spangler was plainly terrified — he trembled visibly at times — and Herold seemed so cowed and helpless that he reminded people of a trapped animal. Dr. Mudd wore a mild, timid look, and Atzerodt somehow contrived to look both hangdog and crafty. But the two defendants who attracted the most attention were Lewis Paine and Mrs. Surratt.

What astounded onlookers about Paine was his dignity, his coolness and his apparent indifference to what was going on in the courtroom. He was guilty of the attack on Seward, he said, and he wished they would "hang him quick" and get it over with. Proudly erect and beautifully muscled, he passed much of his time in the courtroom staring dreamily out of the window. He never wept but he laughed once — when he was requested to try on the hat that he had dropped in Seward's bedroom. It proved to be a perfect fit. Of all the defendants, he was the only one who throughout the trial appeared perfectly at ease.

At the end of the prisoners' row sat Mrs. Surratt, her face concealed behind a heavy black veil. Dressed entirely in black, she would remain motionless for hours on end, except for gently waving a palm-leaf fan through the air; on a few occasions, though, she had to be removed from the courtroom because of faintness.

To make its case against Mary Surratt, the government called nine major witnesses. Two of these — the lodger Louis Weichmann and the Surrattsville tavern-keeper John Lloyd — offered testimony of critical importance. Both men had been threatened by government interrogators and were talking to save their own skins.

Upon returning to Washington after his fruitless search in Canada for John Surratt, Weichmann had been released from custody — only to be summoned into Stanton's presence the following morning. As Weichmann recounted the episode, Stanton had not been so much angry as baffled. "How in the name of common sense," he had inquired, "did you come to make your home with that disloyal Surratt family?" Indeed, recalled Weichmann, Stanton had appeared to be half-apologetic as he "gave me to understand that he would be compelled to put me under lock and key."

The facts were almost certainly different. Weichmann had been thrown into a common cell with 30 other prisoners, among whom was John T. Ford, the owner of Ford's Theatre. The story Ford got from Weichmann was that Stanton had threatened him with the remark that "his hands had as much of the President's blood on them as Booth's." Moreover, even if Stanton had been as mild as Weichmann claimed, others clearly were not. Thus, on May 5, Weichmann wrote from his cell to Colonel Henry Burnett, one of the assistants to the Judge Advocate General in the trial: "You confused and terrified

me so much yesterday that I was almost unable to say anything. For God's Sake do not confound the innocent with the guilty."

John Lloyd had even more cause to be scared out of his wits. By his own admission, he had hidden the weapons given him by John Surratt, thus involving himself more deeply in the assassination plot than some of the defendants. "I am to be shot! I am to be shot!" he had sobbed to his wife at the time of his arrest. As if he were not already frightened enough, Lloyd was interrogated in prison by a certain Colonel Foster, whom he remembered with dread: "He jumps up very quick off his seat, as if very mad, and asked me if I knew what I was guilty of. I told him under the circumstances I did not. He said you are guilty as an accessory to a crime the punishment of which is death."

And so, each of them thoroughly intimidated, Louis Weichmann and John Lloyd made their fateful appearances on the witness stand in the courtroom of the Old Penitentiary. The testimony of both men centered on trips that Mary Surratt had made to the Maryland countryside, one on April 11 and the other on April 14, only hours before the assassination.

According to Weichmann, Mrs. Surratt had told him on the rainy morning of April 11 that she had business in Surrattsville. She asked him to go to the National Hotel to borrow a horse and buggy from Booth. Explaining that he had recently sold his buggy, Booth gave Weichmann $10 to rent one. Weichmann did so, and he and his landlady had set out about 9 a.m. Near Uniontown, they had met Lloyd and Lloyd's sister-in-law driving in the opposite direction. When Lloyd got out of his carriage and came walking over to them, claimed Weichmann, Mrs.

GEORGE ATZERODT
Death by hanging

LEWIS PAINE
Death by hanging

DAVID HEROLD
Death by hanging

DR. SAMUEL MUDD
Life imprisonment

SAMUEL ARNOLD
Life imprisonment

EDMAN SPANGLER
Six years imprisonment

MICHAEL O'LAUGHLIN
Life imprisonment

Surratt "leaned sideways in the buggy, and whispered, as it were, in Mr. Lloyd's ear."

Again, Weichmann testified, on the afternoon of April 14, Mrs. Surratt had asked that he drive her to Surrattsville. As they were about to leave, Booth stopped by for a time to speak privately to Mrs. Surratt. When Mrs. Surratt got in the buggy, she was carrying a package that the actor had apparently given her. It was about six inches in diameter and looked to Weichmann like two or three saucers wrapped up. When Weichmann and Mrs. Surratt left Surrattsville to make the return trip to Washington, she no longer had the mysterious package.

Taken alone, Weichmann's tale of the trips to Surrattsville seemed almost innocuous. One member of the court, General Harris, subsequently wrote that if Mrs. Surratt's fate had depended on what Weichmann said, "not a hair of her head would have been harmed. The man who did the mischief was John M. Lloyd." Nonetheless, Weichmann's testimony was vital to the prosecution, for it dovetailed neatly with that of Lloyd. During their brief conversation on April 11, Lloyd testified, Mrs. Surratt had told him that the carbines he had hidden for John Surratt would be wanted soon. Then, on her April 14 visit to Surrattsville, she had said: "I want you to have those shooting irons ready; there will be parties here tonight who will call for them." On the same visit, she had handed him a pair of field glasses wrapped in paper and two bottles of whiskey to be given to whoever called for them that night.

Mrs. Surratt's youthful lawyers, Aiken and Clampitt, did their best. Pressed about their client's use of the slang expression "shooting irons," which seemed out of char-

acter for a woman who prided herself on her ladylike ways, Lloyd grew confused. He was confident that she had talked of shooting irons on both visits, he declared at first — but then added that he was not so sure. The lawyers cast further doubt on his credibility by getting his sister-in-law to admit that, on the occasion of Mrs. Surratt's April 14 visit, "Mr. Lloyd was very much in liquor, more so than I had ever seen him."

Equally important, the defense lawyers were able to prove that on both the days in question, their client had had perfectly legitimate business affairs that took her to Surrattsville. She had owed several hundred dollars to a Charles Calvert, for land her late husband had purchased but never finished paying off. She had told Calvert that she would be unable to pay him until she in turn received $479, plus interest, that was due her from a man named John Nothey. With Calvert dunning her hard, the beleaguered widow had set out for Surrattsville on April 11 determined to collect from Nothey. However, after talking to him at Lloyd's tavern, she left empty-handed. Then, on April 14, she had received a letter from Calvert implying he meant to go to court for his money. Again Mrs. Surratt had traveled to Surrattsville, but this time she failed to find Nothey. Instead, she left her debtor a message, written for her by Louis Weichmann, that threatened him with a lawsuit.

For whatever it may or may not have been worth, such evidence was swept aside by the passionate closing argument of commissioner John Bingham, who pronounced Mary Surratt every bit as guilty as her son. Plainly, said Bingham, the mother had "instigated and encouraged" the son "to strike this traitorous and murderous blow against his coun-

try." With those words still reverberating in their ears, the officers of the court went into closed session on June 29, where they deliberated the future of Mary Surratt and her fellow defendants.

The commission's first task — deciding the guilt or innocence of each defendant — was quickly accomplished. All but one were convicted of the main charge of "treasonable conspiracy." The exception, Ned Spangler, was found guilty on a lesser charge of aiding and abetting John Wilkes Booth in his flight from Ford's Theatre.

Next the tribunal set the sentences. Spangler was given six years at hard labor. Dr. Mudd, Arnold and O'Laughlin received life imprisonment — though Mudd escaped death by only one vote. Death sentences were imposed on Paine, Herold, Atzerodt

and Mary Surratt. In Mrs. Surratt's case, however, five members of the commission signed a recommendation to President Johnson that he commute her sentence to life imprisonment because of her age and sex.

Both the verdicts and the sentences were kept secret until President Johnson could review and sign the requisite papers.

It so happened that the President was suffering at the time from an ailment described as bilious fever. Not until July 5 did he feel well enough to receive Joseph Holt, who slipped into the White House through a side door. Holt brought with him an abstract of the trial proceedings. Exactly what happened next will never be known. What is certain is that by the end of the session, President Johnson had approved the death sentences of Lewis Paine, David Herold, George Atzerodt —

Federal sentries with fixed bayonets stand guard over fellow soldiers arrested for voicing approval of Lincoln's assassination. These men were forced to wear placards proclaiming them "assassination sympathizers"; others had their heads shaved, or were sentenced to hard labor.

and Mary Surratt. The date of execution was set for July 7, a mere two days ahead.

It was all cut and dried, or so it seemed. Yet there would be a stormy aftermath. Two years later, John Surratt was captured at last, and during his trial a defense lawyer mentioned rumors that a petition of clemency for Mary Surratt had been included in the papers that Holt had showed Johnson. At that, President Johnson ordered the War Department to send him the documents. Sure enough, the petition was among them. Johnson issued a statement saying that he had never seen the recommendation and that he remembered the great reluctance with which he had approved her death. Holt to the end of his days would insist that the President had read, discussed and refused the petition.

In their cells, the prisoners remained ignorant of their fate until the morning of July 6. Shortly before noon, Major General Winfield Scott Hancock, the respected corps commander who was now military commander of the district, and General Hartranft, the prison commandant, walked into the cells of the four condemned to death and read them their sentences. Hours later, Mrs. Surratt's attorneys got the dire news when they heard a newsboy shouting the headlines outside their office. Remembered Clampitt: "So sudden was the shock, so unexpected the result, amazed beyond expression at the celerity of the order, we hardly knew how to proceed."

Yet they tried. That afternoon Clampitt accompanied Anna Surratt to the White House, where the young woman hoped to persuade the President to spare her mother's life. They were referred instead to Joseph Holt, who turned them away. The President, he said, was "immovable" and "You might as well attempt to overthrow this building as to alter his decision."

The next morning, only hours before the executions were scheduled to take place, Anna returned to the White House. Mounting the stairs to the President's second-floor office, she found her way barred by one-time New York Senator Preston King, a close friend of Johnson's, and by Kansas Senator James Lane, a veteran of the Kansas-Missouri guerrilla wars. Throwing herself onto the stairs, Anna wept bitterly. As she lay there, President Johnson's daughter happened to come along. "My poor dear," said Martha Johnson Patterson, "you break my heart, but there is not a thing I can do."

One hope remained. At 2 a.m., the condemned woman's lawyers had roused Judge Alexander Wylie of the District of Columbia Supreme Court from his slumbers and pleaded for an order staying the execution of Mary Surratt. Evidently a man of considerable courage, Wylie had issued a writ of habeas corpus — even while remarking that his action would probably land him in jail.

The effort was useless. At 11:30 that morning, General Hancock appeared bearing an order signed by President Johnson. It suspended the right of habeas corpus.

By then a crowd had begun to gather in the courtyard outside the Washington Arsenal. At 1:15 p.m. on that blistering afternoon, the arsenal door opened and a forlorn little procession emerged. The condemned foursome was led by Mary Surratt, scarcely able to walk and supported by soldiers on either side. Passing close by their own freshly dug graves, each with a raw pine coffin beside it, the prisoners slowly climbed the scaffold.

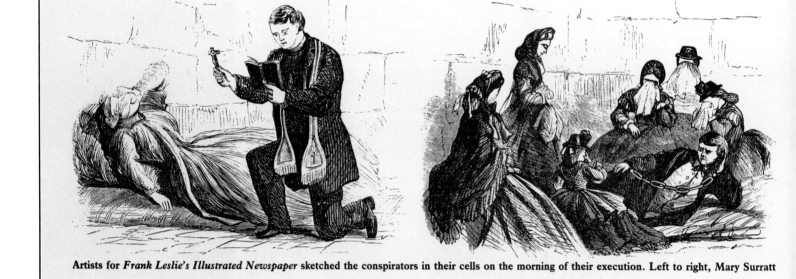

Artists for *Frank Leslie's Illustrated Newspaper* sketched the conspirators in their cells on the morning of their execution. Left to right, Mary Surratt

Chairs had been provided for all the prisoners. A vagrant puff of wind blew off the white straw hat that Lewis Paine was wearing; someone ran to get it for him, but Paine indicated with a gesture that he would no longer be needing a hat.

Until almost that moment, General Hancock, who was in overall charge of the executions, had felt confident that President Johnson would issue a last-minute reprieve for Mrs. Surratt; indeed, he had arranged for a relay of cavalrymen to hasten the merciful message from the White House. Similarly, to save himself the time and trouble of tying the customary seven knots in the woman's noose, hangman Christian Rath had tied only five, since he "fully expected that Mrs. Surratt would never hang."

From the White House, however, came only silence, and Hancock had no choice but to proceed. Mounting the scaffold, he ordered the executioner to get on with his work. "Her too?" asked Rath, indicating Mary Surratt. Her too, nodded Hancock.

As soldiers tied the prisoners' hands behind their backs and placed white hoods over their heads, David Herold trembled violently, his eyes darting about as if he sought some avenue of escape. George Atzerodt summoned a measure of courage. "Goodbye, gentlemen," he cried in his guttural accent,

"may we all meet in the other world." Standing erect on the scaffold, Lewis Paine told his guards, "Mrs. Surratt is innocent. She doesn't deserve to die with the rest of us."

The hangman, who respected Paine's stoicism, put the noose around the big man's neck himself, saying that he wanted Paine "to die quick." Murmured Paine calmly, "You know best."

Finally, a little before 2 p.m., General Hancock clapped his hands three times. At the sound of the third clap, soldiers beneath the scaffold used heavy timbers to knock away the props that supported the hinged traps, and the prisoners plunged down.

Samuel Mudd, Michael O'Laughlin, Ned Spangler and Sam Arnold were transported to one of the earth's most desolate spots: the wildly misnamed Garden Key in the Dry Tortugas, a chain of tiny, sun-bleached, disease-infested islands off the Florida coast. "Oh," cried Mudd upon hearing of his new destination, "there is no hope for me! I cannot live in such a place!"

But live he did, and the horror of the place was perhaps the saving of him. In August of 1867, yellow fever swept the Dry Tortugas, killing, among others, O'Laughlin. When the prison doctor also died, Mudd volunteered to take his place in ministering to

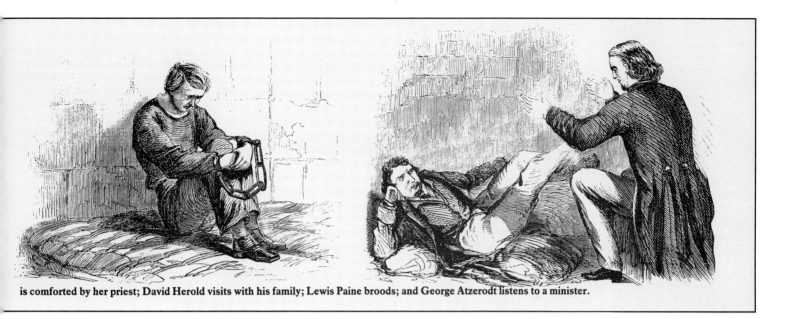
is comforted by her priest; David Herold visits with his family; Lewis Paine broods; and George Atzerodt listens to a minister.

stricken prisoners and guards alike. In gratitude for his services, prison officers later appealed for his release — and in one of his last acts in office, President Johnson signed the papers that freed not only Mudd but Arnold and Spangler as well. By then Spangler was dying of tuberculosis; Mudd took the man into his Maryland home and employed him during the two years he had left to live.

The conspiracy came briefly alive again in the public mind when John Surratt was captured and brought to trial in Washington, two years after his fellow conspirators had been judged and condemned. Hidden by a priest in Canada for several weeks after Lincoln's assassination, Surratt had eventually made his way to Rome, where he had enrolled under an assumed name in the Papal Zouaves. Upon being recognized by an old schoolmate, he had been arrested by order of the Vatican chancellor. While being taken to jail he had escaped, only to turn up first in Naples and then in Egypt, where he had again been recognized and arrested.

Returned to Washington, Surratt was brought to trial on June 10, 1867, for conspiring to murder President Lincoln. This time, however, the case was tried in a civil court with a jury of Surratt's peers. When the jury could not agree on a verdict, the case was dismissed. A second trial was called within a few weeks, and this time the case foundered on questions of procedure. The government had charged Surratt with conspiracy and treason. But, said the defense, the two-year statute of limitations on these charges had run out. Incredibly, the prosecution failed to state that during those years Surratt had been a fugitive from justice. The case was *nolle prossed*, and Surratt was freed. Finding a job in Maryland, he lived quietly until his death at the age of 72, emerging once or twice to offer limp reasons for not having come forth on his mother's behalf.

And what of Edwin M. Stanton, the man who brought retribution to the accused assassins of President Lincoln? He would soon find himself in such bitter opposition to President Johnson's policies toward the defeated South that he would be fired by the President — an act that would help trigger Johnson's impeachment. If Stanton felt any misgivings about the conduct of the conspiracy trial, he never expressed them to the day of his death, Christmas Eve of 1869. By then, thanks to the scalding hatreds inspired both by the Civil War and by the assassination of Lincoln, the long, lamentable process of reconstruction had begun. Its effects would be felt well into the 20th Century.

"We Wish to Hear Their Names No More"

Shortly after 1 p.m. on July 7, 1865, the back door of Washington's Old Penitentiary swung open, and the four condemned conspirators — Mary Surratt, David Herold, George Atzerodt and Lewis Paine — entered a three-acre yard (*right*). Soldiers lounging in the 100° heat snapped to attention, and the spectators huddled closer to the scaffold, which had been hammered together the day before under the direction of the hangman, Captain Christian Rath of the Veteran Reserve Corps.

Accompanied by a small escort of guards and clergymen, the prisoners mounted the 13 steps to the platform, where the grisly task of execution proceeded. Few tears were shed for them. "We wish to hear their names no more," declared a Northern newspaper, "and to be permitted to think of our dead President only as a great and good man and patriot gone to his rest, without associating his name with the names of the wretches who have paid the penalty of their crimes with their worthless lives."

The only photographer authorized to cover the hangings was Alexander Gardner, whose stark pictures appear here and on the following pages.

Soldiers of the 6th Regiment, Veteran Volunteers, stand guard atop a brick wall 20 feet high as spectators linger in the prison yard after witnessing the hangings. Four coffins for the condemned prisoners are stacked in front of the gallows.

Umbrellas provide relief from the sun as Brigadier General John F. Hartranft, standing at the center of the scaffold, reads the order of execution to the prisoners, who are seated in armchairs on either side of him. Mrs. Surratt (*far left*) is being comforted by two priests; next to her, Lewis Paine is partially obscured by the gallows' center beam. At the right of the scaffold, a minister whispers in David Herold's ear and George Atzerodt, his head covered by a white handkerchief, listens attentively to Hartranft. Under the scaffold, soldiers stand ready to knock out the temporary props supporting two hinged trap doors.

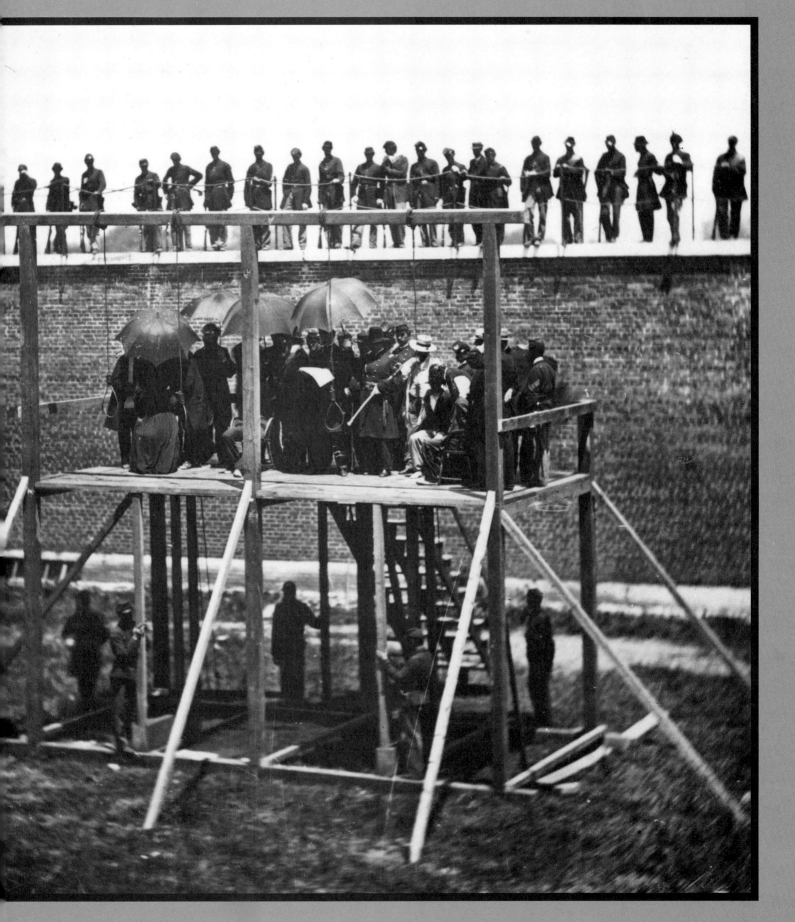

The clergymen's prayers said, the prisoners are prepared for hanging. Captain Rath, wearing a white coat and hat, adjusts a rope around David Herold's neck while another official fixes George Atzerodt's noose. Lewis Paine's arms and legs have been bound with strips of white tent cloth, and he is being fitted with a death cap of the same material. Mrs. Surratt, for whom a last-minute reprieve had been expected, is still seated. "It was with a shudder that I saw an officer gather the ropes tightly three times about her robes and bind her ankles with the cords," one witness wrote. "She half fainted, and sank backwards upon the attendants." Below Mrs. Surratt, Corporal William Coxshall, one of the men assigned to spring the traps, holds onto the supporting timber; the heat and the strain of waiting have made him sick.

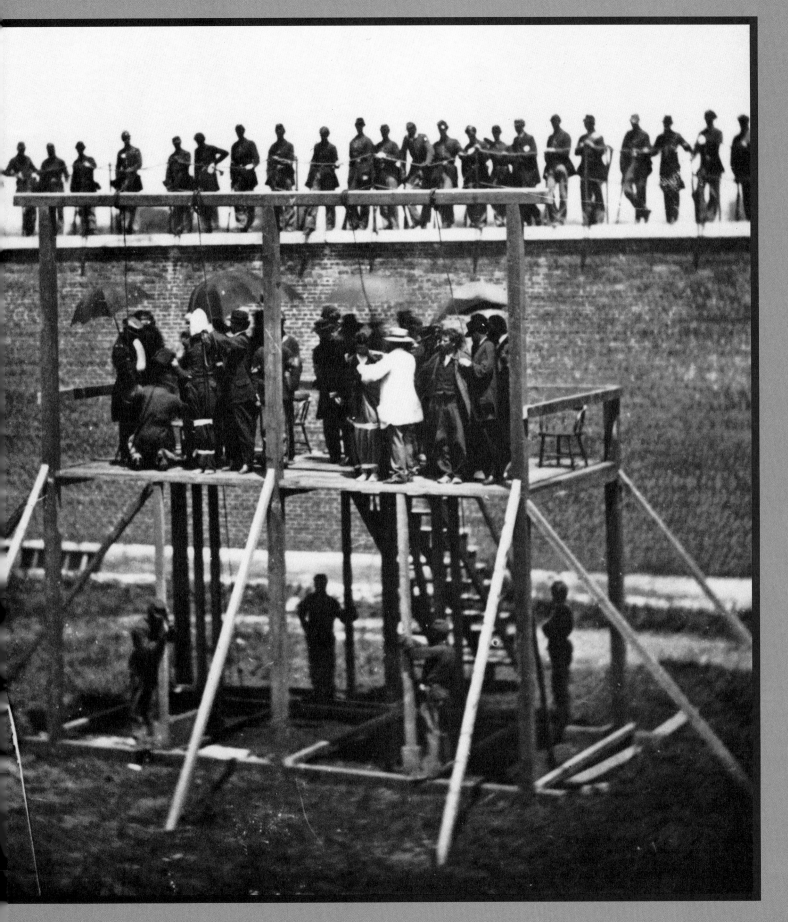

The traps are sprung, and the condemned prisoners drop into open air. "They bounded up again like a ball attached to a rubber band," observed Christian Rath, the hangman, "and then they settled down."

The bodies of the conspirators dangle from the gallows before being cut down, placed in the U.S. Navy equipment boxes *(far right)* that served as their coffins, and

buried near the prison. A bottle containing the name of the occupant was put in each coffin. The gallows and ropes were cut into pieces and distributed as souvenirs.

ACKNOWLEDGMENTS

The editors wish to thank the following individuals and institutions for their valuable assistance in the preparation of this volume: •

Connecticut: West Hartford — Edmund Sullivan, University of Hartford.

Illinois: Springfield — Thomas F. Schwartz, Illinois State Historical Library.

Indiana: Fort Wayne — Mark E. Neely Jr., Louis A. Warren Lincoln Library and Museum. Indianapolis — Carolyn Autry, Indiana Historical Society.

Maine: Boothbay — Franklyn Lenthall, The Boothbay Theatre Museum.

Maryland: Clinton — Laurie Verge, Surratt House & Tavern.

Massachusetts: Cambridge — Martha Mahard, Harvard University College Library.

Michigan: Dearborn — Michael Ettema, Henry Ford Museum and Greenfield Village.

Minnesota: Edina — Floyd E. Risvold.

New York: Chappaqua — Philip B. Kunhardt Jr. New York — Terry Ariano and Mary Ann Smith, Museum of the City of New York; Dr. John K. Lattimer, Columbia Presbyterian Medical Center; Louis Racow, Hampden Booth Theatre Library. Seaford — Richard Sloan.

Pennsylvania: Gettysburg — Mark Katz, Americana Image Gallery.

Rhode Island: Providence — Jennifer B. Lee, John Hay Library, Brown University.

Tennessee: Harrogate — Judy Johnson, Lincoln Museum, Lincoln Memorial University.

Texas: Fort Worth — Donald Dow.

Virginia: Alexandria — Wenda Heilman. McLean — James O. Hall.

Washington, D.C.: Larry Baume, Columbia Historical Society; Barbara Burger, Deborah Edge and staff, Jonathan Heller, Still Pictures Branch, National Archives; Roxanna Deane, Mary Ternes, D.C. Public Library; James Gilreath, Rare Books and Special Collections Division, Library of Congress; Frank Hebblethwaite, Ford's Theatre National Historic Site; Marilyn V. Higgins, Division of Political History, National Museum of American History, Smithsonian Institution; George Hobart, Documentary Photographs, Library of Congress; Eveline Nave, Photoduplication Service, Library of Congress; Nicholas J. Scheetz, Lauinger Library, Georgetown University; Frances D. Turgeon, Kiplinger Washington Collection.

The index for this volume was prepared by Roy Nanovic.

PICTURE CREDITS

Credits from left to right are separated by semicolons, from top to bottom by dashes.

Cover: National Archives Neg. No. 111-B-6135. 2, 3: Map by Peter McGinn. 9: National Portrait Gallery, Smithsonian Institution, Washington, D.C. (NPG.M-81.1). 10: Library of Congress, from *Abraham Lincoln: The War Years*, by Carl Sandburg, published by Harcourt, Brace & World, New York City, 1939. 11: McLellan Lincoln Collection, John Hay Library, Brown University. 12, 13: Library of Congress. 14: Courtesy Frank & Marie-T. Wood Print Collections, Alexandria, Virginia. 15: Library of Congress. 16: Harvard Theatre Collection, Harvard University, copied by Henry Groskinsky. 17: Handy Studios, Washington, D.C., from *The Mad Booths of Maryland*, by Stanley Kimmel, published by The Bobbs-Merrill Company, New York City, 1940. 19: Richard J. S. and Kellie O. Gutman Collection, from *John Wilkes Booth Himself*, Hired Hand Press, Dover, Massachusetts, 1979; courtesy Robert L. Keesler, copied by Robert A. Grove. 22, 23: Courtesy Frank & Marie-T. Wood Print Collections, Alexandria, Virginia; from *Battles and Leaders of the Civil War*, Vol. 2, published by The Century Company, New York City, 1887; from *Perley's Reminiscences of Sixty Years in the National Metropolis*, Vol. 2, by Ben: Perley Poore, published by Hubbard Brothers, Philadelphia, Pennsylvania, 1886(2); Martin Luther King Memorial Library, Washingtoniana Division, Washington, D.C.; from Civil War Times Illustrated *Album Illustrating the Assassination of Abraham Lincoln*, published by Stackpole Books, Harrisburg, Pennsylvania, 1965 — National Park Service (NPS), Ford's Theatre, Washington, D.C.(2) — National Theatre Archives, Washington, D.C.; from *Perley's Reminiscences of Sixty Years in the National Metropolis*, Vol. 2, by Ben: Perley Poore, published by Hubbard Brothers, Philadelphia, Pennsylvania, 1886 — Library of Congress; Martin Luther King Memorial Library, Washingtoniana Division, Washington, D.C.(3). Map by Fred Holz. 25: National Archives Negs. Nos. 111-B-6185; 111-B-1161 — Library of Congress(4). 26: Martin Luther King Memorial Library, Washingtoniana Division, Washington, D.C.; courtesy the Kunhardt Collection, from *Twenty Days*, by Dorothy Meserve Kunhardt and Philip B. Kunhardt Jr., published by Harper & Row, New York City, 1965 — National Archives Neg. No. 111-B-1138. 28, 29: National Archives Neg. No. 66-G-22B-1. 30: The Hampden-Booth Theatre Library at The Players. 31: Theatre Collection, Museum of the City of New York. 32: Theatre Collection, Museum of the City of New York, except right, The Hampden-Booth Theatre Library at The Players. 33: Theatre Collection, Museum of the City of New York, photographed by Henry Groskinsky; The Hampden-Booth Theatre Library at The Players. 34: Courtesy Richard J. S. and Kellie O. Gutman Collection, from *John Wilkes Booth Himself*, Hired Hand Press, Dover, Massachusetts, 1979; courtesy John K. Lattimer, M.D., photographed by Henry Groskinsky; courtesy Terry Alford, photographed by Robert A. Grove. 35: Courtesy Richard J. S. and Kellie O. Gutman Collection; courtesy of the Kimmel Collection, Merl Kelce Library, The University of Tampa; The Hampden-Booth Theatre Library at The Players; Theatre Collection, Museum of the City of New York; The Hampden-Booth Theatre Library at The Players; courtesy of the Kimmel Collection, Merl Kelce Library, The University of Tampa. 36, 37: Harvard Theatre Collection, Harvard University; Theatre Collection, Museum of the City of New York; Harvard Theatre Collection, Harvard University, photographed by Henry Groskinsky. 39: Louis A. Warren Lincoln Library and Museum, Fort Wayne, Indiana, photographed by Scott Simpson. 41: Library of Congress. 42: Watercolor by A. Meyer, Library of Congress. 43: Courtesy Floyd E. Risvold Collection. 45: Lloyd Ostendorf Collection, Dayton, Ohio. 46: National Museum of American History, Smithsonian Institution, Washington, D.C. — Lloyd Ostendorf Collection, Dayton, Ohio. 47: The Western Reserve Historical Society, Cleveland, Ohio. 48: Louis A. Warren Lincoln Library and Museum, Fort Wayne, Indiana, photographed by Scott Simpson. 50: Library of Congress. 51: Richard J. S. and Kellie O. Gutman Collection. 52: Drawing by Edwin Forbes, Kean Archives, Philadelphia, Pennsylvania. 55: Library of Congress; from a private collection. 56, 57: Library of Congress. 58: Painting by Thomas Nast, courtesy The Union League Club of New York, photographed by Paulus Leeser. 60: Harvard Theatre Collection, Harvard University; Richard J. S. and Kellie O. Gutman Collection, from *John Wilkes Booth Himself*, Hired Hand Press, Dover, Massachusetts, 1979(2). 61: The Hampden-Booth Theatre Library at The Players. 62, 63: Richard J. S. and Kellie O. Gutman Collection, from *John Wilkes Booth Himself*, Hired Hand Press, Dover, Massachusetts, 1979(3) — Richard J. S. and Kellie O. Gutman Collection(3). 65: NPS, Ford's Theatre, Washington, D.C., photographed by Edward Owen. 66: Louis A. Warren Lincoln Library and Museum, Fort Wayne, Indiana, photographed by Scott Simpson. 68, 69: Library of Congress. 70: Harvard Theatre Collection, Harvard University, copied by Henry Groskinsky. 72: Courtesy John K. Lattimer, M.D. 73: Harvard Theatre Collection, Harvard University, photographed by Henry Groskinsky; Louis A. Warren Lincoln Library and Museum, Fort Wayne, Indiana — courtesy the Kunhardt Collection, from *Twenty Days*, by Dorothy Meserve Kunhardt and Philip B. Kunhardt Jr., published by Harper & Row, New York City, 1965. 75: Library of Congress. 77: National Archives Neg. No. 111-B-2040; Library of Congress. 78: Courtesy Lloyd Ostendorf Collection, Dayton, Ohio. 80: NPS, Ford's Theatre, Washington, D.C., photographed by Edward Owen, except right, The Abraham Lincoln Museum, Lincoln Memorial University, photographed by Charles Warren. 81: Library of Congress, photographed by Michael Latil, except top left, National Museum of American History, Smithsonian Institution, Washington, D.C., photographed by Dane Penland. 81: From the Collections of Henry Ford Museum and Greenfield Village, No. 11-A-35(A). 84: Diagram by Fred Holz. 85-87: Courtesy Frank & Marie-T. Wood Print Collections, Alexandria, Virginia. 88, 89: Courtesy Frank & Marie-T. Wood Print Collections, Alexandria, Virginia, except center, NPS, Ford's Theatre, Washington, D.C., photographed by Edward Owen. 90, 91: Courtesy Frank & Marie-T. Wood Print Collections, Alexandria, Virginia. 93: McLellan Lincoln Collection, John Hay Library, Brown University. 94, 95: Painting by Carl Bersch, NPS, Ford's Theatre, Washington, D.C., photographed by Edward Owen. 96: Courtesy Frank & Marie-T. Wood Print Collections, Alexandria, Virginia. 97: Courtesy John K. Lattimer, M.D., photographed by Henry Groskinsky; from *The Assassination and History of the Conspiracy*, reprinted by Hobbs, Dorman & Company, New York City, 1965. 99: National Archives Neg. No. 111-B-4214. 100: McLellan Lincoln Collection, John Hay Library, Brown University. 101: Courtesy Frank & Marie-T. Wood Print Collections, Alexandria, Virginia, photographed by Mazyar Parvaresh. 102, 103: Courtesy Frank & Marie-T. Wood Print Collections, Alexandria, Virginia; courtesy Lloyd Ostendorf Collection, Dayton, Ohio. 105: Eugene Boss Collection, Special Collections Division, Georgetown University Library, photographed by Robert A. Grove. 106, 107: Library of Congress, inset courtesy C. Paul Loane. 109: NPS, Ford's Theatre, Washington, D.C., photographed by Edward Owen; courtesy Richard D. Mudd, M.D. 111: McLellan Lincoln Collection, John Hay Library, Brown University. 112: Kean

Archives, Philadelphia, Pennsylvania. 113: Map by Fred Holz. 114, 115: Courtesy James O. Hall. 116: Theatre Collection, Museum of the City of New York. 118, 119: Library of Congress(2) — courtesy Donald P. Dow, photographed by David Buffington; courtesy Frank & Marie-T. Wood Print Collections, Alexandria, Virginia. 120, 121: Courtesy Frank & Marie-T. Wood Print Collections, Alexandria, Virginia; courtesy John K. Lattimer, M.D., photographed by Henry Groskinsky; courtesy the Kunhardt Collection, from *Twenty Days*, by Dorothy Meserve Kunhardt and Philip B. Kunhardt Jr., published by Harper & Row, New York City, 1965 — courtesy the Kunhardt Collection, from *Twenty Days*, by Dorothy Meserve Kunhardt and Philip B. Kunhardt Jr., published by Harper & Row, New York City, 1965; Museum of the City of New York. 122, 123: Courtesy The New-York Historical Society; Museum of the City of New York; courtesy the Kunhardt Collection, from *Twenty Days*, by Dorothy Meserve Kunhardt and Philip B. Kunhardt Jr., published by Harper & Row, New York City, 1965 — Illinois State Historical Library, Springfield; The Abraham Lincoln Museum, Lincoln Memorial University, photographed by Charles War-

ren. 124, 125: Courtesy the Kunhardt Collection, from *Twenty Days*, by Dorothy Meserve Kunhardt and Philip B. Kunhardt Jr., published by Harper & Row, New York City, 1965; Illinois State Historical Library, Springfield — courtesy Donald P. Dow, photographed by David Buffington; courtesy the Kunhardt Collection, from *Twenty Days*, by Dorothy Meserve Kunhardt and Philip B. Kunhardt Jr., published by Harper & Row, New York City, 1965. 126, 127: Chicago Historical Society Neg. No. ICHi-11252; Library of Congress — Eugene Boss Collection, Special Collections Division, Georgetown University Library, photographed by Robert A. Grove(2); courtesy Ed Steers. 128, 129: Courtesy the Kunhardt Collection, from *Twenty Days*, by Dorothy Meserve Kunhardt and Philip B. Kunhardt Jr., published by Harper & Row, New York City, 1965, except bottom right, McLellan Lincoln Collection, John Hay Library, Brown University. 130: Illinois State Historical Library, Springfield — courtesy Frank & Marie-T. Wood Print Collections, Alexandria, Virginia. 131: Courtesy Donald P. Dow, photographed by David Buffington — Illinois State Historical Library, Springfield. 133: Courtesy John K. Lattimer, M.D., photographed by

Henry Groskinsky. 134, 135: Courtesy Donald P. Dow, photographed by David Buffington. 136: Courtesy Frank & Marie-T. Wood Print Collections, Alexandria, Virginia. 137: Kean Archives, Philadelphia, Pennsylvania. 138, 139: NPS, Ford's Theatre, Washington, D.C., photographed by Edward Owen. 141: NPS, Ford's Theatre, Washington, D.C. 142: National Archives Neg. No. 111-B-203 — Library of Congress; courtesy Floyd E. Risvold Collection. 143, 144: Library of Congress. 146, 147: Insets, National Museum of American History, Smithsonian Institution, Washington, D.C., photographed by Dane Penland; courtesy Frank & Marie-T. Wood Print Collections, Alexandria, Virginia. 149: Library of Congress. 151: National Museum of American History, Smithsonian Institution, Washington, D.C., photographed by Dane Penland. 152, 153: Courtesy Frank & Marie-T. Wood Print Collections, Alexandria, Virginia. 156: Drawings by Lew Wallace, Lew Wallace Collection, Indiana Historical Society, Indianapolis. 158: Courtesy Bill Turner. 160, 161: Courtesy Frank & Marie-T. Wood Print Collections, Alexandria, Virginia. 162-167: Library of Congress. 168, 169: Courtesy D. Mark Katz. 170, 171: Library of Congress.

BIBLIOGRAPHY

Books

Arnold, Samuel Bland, *Defence and Prison Experiences of a Lincoln Conspirator: Statements and Autobiographical Notes.* Hattiesburg, Mississippi: The Book Farm, 1943.

Baker, L. C., *History of the United States Secret Service.* Philadelphia: L. C. Baker, 1867.

Bishop, Jim, *The Day Lincoln Was Shot.* New York: Harper & Brothers, 1955.

Bryan, George S., *The Great American Myth.* New York: Carrick & Evans, 1940.

Buckingham, J. E., Sr., *Reminiscences and Souvenirs of the Assassination of Abraham Lincoln.* Washington, D.C.: Press of Rufus H. Darby, 1894.

Campbell, Helen Jones, *Confederate Courier.* New York: St. Martin's Press, 1964.

Catton, Bruce, *Grant Takes Command.* Boston: Little, Brown and Company, 1969.

Civil War Times Illustrated, *Album Illustrating the Assassination of Abraham Lincoln.* Harrisburg, Pennsylvania: Stackpole Books, 1965.

Clarke, Asia Booth, *The Unlocked Book: A Memoir of John Wilkes Booth.* New York: Benjamin Blom, 1971.

Conrad, Thomas Nelson, *The Rebel Scout: A Thrilling History of Scouting Life in the Southern Army.* Washington, D.C.: The National Publishing Company, 1904.

Cottrell, John, *Anatomy of an Assassination.* London: Frederick Muller, 1966.

Crook, William H., *Through Five Administrations: Reminiscences of Colonel William H. Crook, Body-Guard to President Lincoln.* Comp. and ed. by Margarita Spalding Gerry. New York: Harper & Brothers, 1910.

Eisenschiml, Otto, *Why Was Lincoln Murdered?* Boston: Little, Brown and Company, 1937.

Foote, Shelby, *Red River to Appomattox.* Vol. 3 of *The Civil War: A Narrative.* New York: Random House, 1974.

Goff, John S., *Robert Todd Lincoln: A Man in His Own Right.* Norman: University of Oklahoma Press, 1969.

Gutman, Richard J. S., and Kellie O. Gutman, *John Wilkes Booth Himself.* Dover, Massachusetts: Hired Hand Press, 1979.

Hall, James O., *John Wilkes Booth Escape Route.* Clinton,

Maryland: The Surratt Society, 1980.

Hanchett, William, *The Lincoln Murder Conspiracies.* Urbana: University of Illinois Press, 1983.

Johnson, Byron Berkeley, *Abraham Lincoln and Boston Corbett, with Personal Recollections of Each; John Wilkes Booth and Jefferson Davis: A True Story of Their Capture.* Waltham, Massachusetts: Published by the author, 1914.

Jones, Thomas A., *J. Wilkes Booth.* Chicago: Laird & Lee, 1893.

The Junior League of Washington, *An Illustrated History: The City of Washington.* Ed. by Thomas Froncek. New York: Alfred A. Knopf, 1981.

Kimmel, Stanley, *The Mad Booths of Maryland.* New York: Dover Publications, 1969.

Kunhardt, Dorothy Meserve, and Philip B. Kunhardt Jr., *Twenty Days.* New York: Harper & Row, 1965.

Lamon, Ward Hill, *Recollections of Abraham Lincoln: 1847-1865.* Ed. by Dorothy Lamon Teillard. Washington, D.C.: Published by the editor, 1911.

Lattimer, John K., M.D., *Kennedy and Lincoln: Medical and Ballistic Comparisons of Their Assassinations.* New York: Harcourt Brace Jovanovich, 1980.

Lee, Richard M., *Mr. Lincoln's City: An Illustrated Guide to the Civil War Sites of Washington.* McLean, Virginia: EPM Publications, 1981.

Leech, Margaret, *Reveille in Washington: 1860-1865.* New York: Harper & Brothers, 1941.

Lomask, Milton, *Andrew Johnson: President on Trial.* New York: Farrar, Straus and Cudahy, 1960.

Long, E. B., with Barbara Long, *The Civil War Day by Day: An Almanac 1861-1865.* Garden City, New York: Doubleday & Company, 1971.

McBride, Robert W., *Lincoln's Body Guard.* Indianapolis: Indiana Historical Society, 1911.

McFeely, William S., *Grant: A Biography.* New York: W. W. Norton & Company, 1981.

Mellon, James, comp. and ed., *The Face of Lincoln.* New York: The Viking Press, 1979.

Mudd, Samuel A., *The Life of Dr. Samuel A. Mudd.* Ed. by Nettie Mudd. Linden, Tennessee: Continental Book Company, 1975 (reprint of 1960 edition).

Neely, Mark E., Jr., *The Abraham Lincoln Encyclopedia.* New York: McGraw-Hill Book Company, 1982.

Nevins, Allan, *The Emergence of Lincoln.* Vol. 2 of *Prologue to Civil War: 1859-1861.* New York: Charles Scribner's Sons, 1950.

Nicolay, John G., *A Short Life of Abraham Lincoln: Condensed from Nicolay & Hay's Abraham Lincoln, a History.* New York: The Century Company, 1904.

Oates, Stephen B., *With Malice toward None: The Life of Abraham Lincoln.* New York: Harper & Row, 1977.

Oldroyd, Osborn H., *The Assassination of Abraham Lincoln.* Washington, D.C.: O. H. Oldroyd, 1901.

Olszewski, George J.:
House Where Lincoln Died: Furnishing Study. Washington, D.C.: United States Department of the Interior, National Park Service, Division of History, 1967.
Restoration of Ford's Theatre. Washington, D.C.: United States Department of the Interior, National Park Service, National Capital Region, 1963.

Pitman, Benn., *The Assassination of President Lincoln and Trial of the Conspirators.* Cincinnati: Moore, Wilstach and Baldwin, 1865.

Poore, Ben: Perley, *Perley's Reminiscences of Sixty Years in the National Metropolis.* Vol. 2. Philadelphia: Hubbard Brothers, 1886.

Poore, Ben: Perley, ed., *The Conspiracy Trial for the Murder of the President.* 3 vols. Boston: J. E. Tilton and Company, 1865-1866.

Randall, Ruth Painter, *Lincoln's Sons.* Boston: Little, Brown and Company, 1955.

Roscoe, Theodore, *The Web of Conspiracy.* Englewood Cliffs, New Jersey: Prentice-Hall, 1959.

Ruggles, Eleanor, *Prince of Players: Edwin Booth.* New York: W. W. Norton & Company, 1953.

Samples, Gordon, *Lust for Fame: The Stage Career of John Wilkes Booth.* Jefferson, North Carolina: McFarland & Company, 1982.

Sandburg, Carl, *Abraham Lincoln: The War Years.* Vols. 1 and 4. New York: Harcourt, Brace & World, 1939.

Searcher, Victor, *The Farewell to Lincoln.* New York: Abingdon Press, 1965.

Seward, Frederick W., *Reminiscences of a War-Time Statesman and Diplomat: 1830-1915*. New York: G. P. Putnam's Sons, 1916.

Shaw, Dale, *Titans of the American Stage: Edwin Forrest, the Booths, the O'Neills*. Philadelphia: The Westminster Press, 1971.

Thomas, Benjamin P., *Abraham Lincoln: A Biography*. New York: Alfred A. Knopf, 1952.

Thomas, Benjamin P., and Harold M. Hyman, *Stanton: The Life and Times of Lincoln's Secretary of War*. New York: Alfred A. Knopf, 1962.

Townsend, Geo. Alfred, *Campaigns of a Non-Combatant*. New York: Blelock & Company, 1982 (reprint of 1866 edition).

Weichmann, Louis J., *A True History of the Assassination of Abraham Lincoln and of the Conspiracy of 1865*. Ed. by Floyd E. Risvold. New York: Alfred A. Knopf, 1975.

Welles, Gideon, *Diary of Gideon Welles*. Vol. 2. Boston: Houghton Mifflin Company, 1911.

Wilson, Francis, *John Wilkes Booth*. Boston: Houghton Mifflin Company, 1929.

Other Sources

Ashmun, George C., "Recollections of a Peculiar Service." *The Magazine of History with Notes and Queries*. January 1906.

The Boston Herald. "John Wilkes Booth." January 10, 1890.

Daily Morning Chronicle. Washington, D.C., April 18, 1865.

Ford, John T., "Behind the Curtain of a Conspiracy." *The North American Review*. April 1889.

Hall, James O., "A Noted Author Explains the Mystery of Lincoln's Guard." *The Maryland Independent*. July 19, 1978.

Johnson, Patricia Carley, ed., " 'I Have Supped Full on Horrors' from Fanny Seward's Diary." *American Heritage*. October 1959.

Katz, D. Mark:
"Booth's First Attempt." *Incidents of the War*. Spring 1986.

"Christian Rath: The Executioner." *Incidents of the War*. Spring 1986.

Kauffman, Michael W., *Booth, Republicanism, and the Lincoln Assassination*. Thesis. December 1980.

Kunhardt, Dorothy Meserve, and Philip B. Kunhardt Jr., "Assassination!" *American Heritage*. April 1965.

Lincoln Lore. "Major Rathbone and Miss Harris Guests of the Lincolns in the Ford's Theatre Box." August 1971.

Loyal Legion Historical Journal. "The First Physician to Reach President Lincoln after His Assassination." February 1974.

The National Archives, *Voluntary Statement of David E. Herold Made before the Honorable John A. Bingham, Special Judge Advocate on the 27th Day of April, 1865*. Microfilm.

The National Tribune. "The Death of J. Wilkes Booth." March 1880.

Steers, Edward, Jr., *The Escape and Capture of George A. Atzerodt*. Private papers. No date.

Steers, Edward, Jr., and Joan L. Chaconas, *The Escape & Capture of John Wilkes Booth*. Marker Tours, 1985.

INDEX

Numerals in italics indicate an illustration of the subject mentioned.